HaynesXtreme
Customizing

Ford Focus

Haynes Publishing Group
Sparkford Nr Yeovil
Somerset BA22 7JJ
England

Haynes North America, Inc
861 Lawrence Drive
Newbury Park
California 91320 USA

Acknowledgements

Cover photos: Focuses shown on the front cover owned by Alfonso Schessler, Robert Farrell and APC (American Products Company). Our sincere thanks to the following Focus owners who allowed us to photograph their outstanding cars for use throughout this book:

APC (American Products Company)
Robert Farrell
Andrew Green

Alfonso Schessler
Ryan Eberhardt
Simon Oliver

© Haynes North America, Inc. 2004
With permission from J.H. Haynes & Co. Ltd.

All rights reserved. No part of this book may be reproduced or transmitted in any form of by any means, electronic or mechanical, including photocopying, recording or by any information storage or retrieval system, without permission in writing from the copyright holder.

ISBN 1 56392 529 X
Library of Congress Control Number 2004100702

Printed by J H Haynes & Co Ltd,
Sparkford, Yeovil, Somerset BA22 7JJ, England.

While every attempt is made to ensure that the information in this manual is correct, no liability can be accepted by the authors or publishers for loss, damage, or injury caused by any errors in, or omissions from, the information given.

"Ford" and the Ford logo are registered trademarks of Ford Motor Company. Ford Motor Company is not a sponsor or affiliate of Haynes Publishing Group or Haynes North America, Inc. and is not a contributor to the content of this manual.

04-200

Be careful and know the law!

1 Advice on safety procedures and precautions is contained throughout this manual, and more specifically within the Safety section towards the back of this book. You are strongly recommended to note these comments, and to pay close attention to any instructions that may be given by the parts supplier.

2 Haynes recommends that vehicle modification should only be undertaken by individuals with experience of vehicle mechanics; if you are unsure as to how to go about the modification, advice should be sought from a competent and experienced individual. Any questions regarding modification should be addressed to the product manufacturer concerned, and not to Haynes, nor the vehicle manufacturer.

3 The instructions in this manual are followed at the risk of the reader who remains fully and solely responsible for the safety, roadworthiness and legality of his/her vehicle. Thus Haynes is giving only non-specific advice in this respect.

4 When modifying a car it is important to bear in mind the legal responsibilities placed on the owners, drivers and modifiers of cars. If you or others modify the car you drive, you and they can be held legally liable for damages or injuries that may occur as a result of the modifications.

5 The safety of any alteration and its compliance with construction and use regulations should be checked before a modified vehicle is sold as it may be an offense to sell a vehicle which is not roadworthy.

6 Any advice provided is correct to the best of our knowledge at the time of publication, but the reader should pay particular attention to any changes of specification to the vehicles, or parts, which can occur without notice.

7 Alterations to a vehicle should be disclosed to insurers and licensing authorities, and legal advice taken from the police, vehicle testing centers, or appropriate regulatory bodies.

8 Some of the procedures shown in this manual will vary from model to model; not all procedures are applicable to all models. Readers should not assume that the vehicle manufacturer has given their approval to the modifications.

9 Neither Haynes nor the manufacturer give any warranty as to the safety of a vehicle after alterations, such as those contained in this book, have been made. Haynes will not accept liability for any economic loss, damage to property or death and personal injury other than in respect to injury or death resulting directly from Haynes' negligence.

Contents

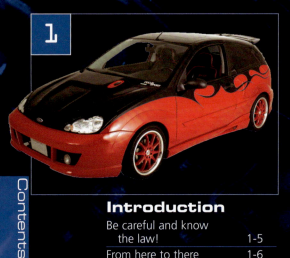

1 Introduction
Be careful and know
   the law!   1-5
From here to there   1-6
Choosing a tuner   1-8
The bad with the good   1-10
A blast through the past   1-12

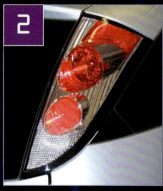

2 Body and exterior
The Ultimate Detail   2-1
De-badging   2-5
Aftermarket mirrors   2-7
Custom headlights   2-9

Aftermarket taillight
   assemblies   2-11
Install a custom grille   2-13
Aerodynamic body kits   2-16
Carbon fiber hoods   2-21
Neon lighting   2-23

6 Suspension
Suspension terms   6-4
Shock absorbers/struts
   and coil springs   6-6
Coilovers   6-11
Rear suspension   6-12
Air suspension   6-16
Nasty side effects   6-17
Strut brace   6-18
Installing stabilizer bars   6-19
Understeer and oversteer   6-21

7 Brakes
Grooved and drilled discs   7-2
Uprated discs and pads   7-3
Painting calipers   7-7
Painting drums   7-9

8 Engine Performance
Engine compartment
   dress-up   8-2
Modifying exhaust   8-12
Turbochargers   8-19
Superchargers   8-23

Custom Painting

How to choose a good paint and body shop	3-2
Vinyl graphics	3-4

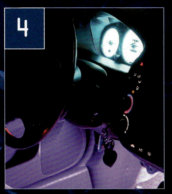

Interiors

Custom styling rings	4-2
Shift lever knobs	4-3
Custom pedals	4-6
Custom floormats	4-8
Neon lighting	4-9

Interior trim	4-12
Gauge face upgrade	4-16
Installing aftermarket gauges	4-21
Bucket seats	4-23
Window tinting	4-26

Wheels and tires

Choosing wheels	5-1
Choosing tires	5-6
Gallery of Wheels	5-8

Nitrous Oxide	8-26
Induction systems	8-29
Computers and chips	8-34
Ignitions systems	8-38
Valvetrain Modifications	8-42
Fuel system	8-46
Race and Live!	8-48

In-Car Entertainment

In-dash receivers and players	9-2
Speakers	9-4
Amplifiers	9-8
Choosing the right amp	9-9
Subwoofer	9-10
Video	9-14

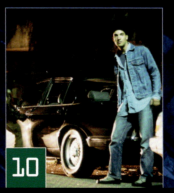

Security

Alarms	10-1
Alarm installation	10-3
Remote power locks	10-6

Safety first!	
Glossary	11-2
Source list	11-7
Haynes list	11-9

From **here . . .**

Ever been to a car show? You'll see the racer with grease under his fingernails, bent over his hood, adjusting his turbo wastegate. You'll see the themed car with matching colors (even under the hood) with a mirror-like paint job reflecting its neon lights. You'll see the rolling sound cannons, with beautifully integrated audio systems, blasting at Richter-scale levels. But you'll also see the daily-driven street cars with custom wheels, body kits and graphics that make them stand out from the other snore-mobiles in the neighborhood. This is truly diversity. And there is no "right" way to customize a car.

. . . to **there**

It seems our cars reflect our personalities, and that's the way it should be. If you're the "all-business" type, you'll probably not care much about your paint job and put the money you save into your engine. For others, looks and appearance are more important, but few of us have the money to "do it all." It's best to figure out what's most important to you and do that first. Look at the number of "unfinished" cars at any show; it illustrates how trying to do it all at once can backfire, especially when you run out of time and money. Most experienced car builders will plan "stages" of modification, each of which can be completed in relatively short periods of time. So, for example, you can get your paint job and graphics, then take some time to save up for your 12-second engine. In the meantime, you can enjoy driving a great-looking car. A die-hard racer might want to do it in reverse, but the principle is the same: it's best not to take on too much at once, unless of course you're the type who wants it all and wants it now - which isn't necessarily a bad thing either.

Choosing a Tuner

Maybe you've already installed some bolt-on parts or done a tune-up or two before you bought this book. Good. You're not totally clueless! You'll be able to install a lot of bolt-on performance goodies with nothing more than the instructions in this book and the right tools. But when your modifications start affecting driveability (rough idle, loss of low-end power, emissions, noise, etc.), turning a stock Focus into a performance machine will get complicated. That's when you'll need to start looking for help. Sometimes you can find the answers in technical articles in enthusiast magazines or in aftermarket books like this one. Theory is a vital part of the learning process, but it's no substitute for practical knowledge, which can only be gained through lots of experience. So at some point you'll need help from someone who knows how everything under the hood works as a system, how each sub-system is interdependent with and affects every other sub-system. Someone, in short, who's already got The Big Picture. We call this person a tuner.

What kind of tuner are you looking for?

Some "tuners" just sell high-performance hardware. They know something about the speed equipment that they sell and some of them might even install it for you. But they don't offer custom tuning services such as machining, welding, fabricating and technical advice. In the early stages of a project (when you're upgrading wheels, tires, brakes, suspension and installing other bolt-on high-performance modifications) one of these tuners might be adequate if you have the mechanical ability and the tools to do your own work. But be realistic about your skills. Some bolt-on mods are expensive, and could be damaged or ruined, or could damage or ruin something else (like the engine!) if incorrectly installed.

Other tuners provide technical help to customers, sell them the stuff that they need to improve their Focus' performance, then install it. These tuners can also make any necessary modifications for customers who need help. If your mechanical ability and tools are limited, find a full-service tuner and leave the mail-order emporiums to more mechanically inclined customers. What you need is someone who can serve as your technical guru and help you reach your performance goals by doing some or all of the work for you. Beginners often waste thousands of dollars on inappropriate modifications because they don't take into consideration how one mod affects another. A "full-service" tuner will make sure that you avoid screw-ups by helping you make good decisions on expensive upgrades that require some planning.

Does the tuner know what he's talking about?

To the tuner, there are just two kinds of experiences: good experiences and . . . learning experiences. When a modification works, it's a good experience. When it doesn't, it's a learning experience. A good tuner isn't afraid to make mistakes, but he doesn't repeat those mistakes. He learns from them and moves on.

Good tuners use their own vehicles, not customers' cars, to research and develop new products and services. If you decide to work with a tuner who intends to use your Focus as a test-bed for new ideas or products, make sure that you get compensated for this service in kind with free or discounted parts and labor.

Ask a prospective tuner about his educational background, experience and training. A novice tuner looking for new customers might feel threatened by such questions and might fudge the truth a bit. But an experienced tuner won't. Besides, if you're going to spend thousands of dollars at this establishment, you need to judge for yourself whether the "tuner" standing before you is really qualified to modify your Focus or tell you how to do it. Did he start out taking auto shop classes at a local high school or study automotive technology at a local community college? Did he work for or own an independent garage? Does he have dealership experience? Is he a certified ASE (Automotive Service Excellence) technician or, even better, an ASE-certified Master Automotive Technician (CMAT)? Did he ever work for a professional motorsports team? His answers to these questions will tell you whether this tuner has devoted a chunk of his life to the automotive field, or whether he's simply out to make a buck.

Some people will tell you that tuning is art, while others say that it's science. But it's neither. Tuning is engineering. Not that one needs a degree in mechanical engineering to become a successful tuner. Most tuners probably aren't "real" engineers. But the good ones do have engineering minds: they understand the complexities of modern automotive technology well enough to define a problem in engineering terms, and then solve it the way an engineer would. A good tuner can back up his advice with sound data, and will be happy to show it to you.

Some of the best tuners gained their special knowledge and skills working for a manufacturer as an engineer or technician or while turning wrenches for a factory racing team. A former factory employee might not only have vast experience with the car you want to modify, he might also maintain some "backdoor," i.e. unofficial, relationship with the factory. Such connections often enable tuners to gain insights into the mysterious inner workings of the engine management system and other esoteric subjects that are unavailable to their competitors.

Does the tuner do the work on time?

Patience is a must when you're putting together a project vehicle with a tuner's help. Still, nobody wants a tuner who is unable or unwilling to deliver goods or services in a timely manner, particularly if the project vehicle is also the daily driver. Ideally, it's a good idea to have a back-up car as a daily driver.

Is the tuner easy to get along with?

Most tuners are helpful and supportive. But some are eccentrics or egomaniacs. This is probably unavoidable in a field that's filled with self-made, self-promoting small businessmen whose success is tied to their accomplishments. If you find that your tuner is patronizing or talking down to you, lecturing you or grumbling about the stupidity of other customers and/or his competitors, get rid of him. You want results, not therapy. A truly hard-working professional doesn't have the time to talk trash about his customers or fellow tuners. He's too busy taking care of business.

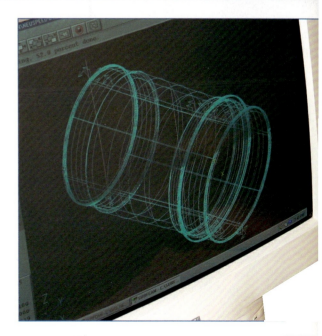

The Bad with the Good

Customizing your car can get complicated in a hurry. What the manufacturers of high-performance and custom parts don't tell you is that there's usually a price to be paid for each "upgrade" you decide to make. For example, if you install big wheels and low-profile tires, be ready for a slightly rougher ride and be sure to stay away from potholes and curbs, since these wheels damage easily. If you install an intake tube, you're going to start hearing the air flowing into your engine (is that a good thing or a bad thing?). If it's a cold-air intake, you're going to have to watch out for deep puddles, or you might wind up with water in your engine (definitely a bad thing). If you lower your car, you're more likely to damage your suspension or destroy a tire from "fender rub." And speed bumps will become your worst enemy. Well, you get the idea. Your Focus was extremely well designed as it came from the factory. It was designed to provide long life, a comfortable ride and excellent fuel economy. These are all attributes we'd like to keep, if possible. So talk to as many people as you can who've actually done the modifications you're planning. Chances are they'll tell you some of the drawbacks that didn't show up in the magazine ad. And, on the other hand, they may let you know about some pleasant surprises they discovered after adding some custom pieces. Sometimes, you just don't know for sure, which is why you need to go in prepared to accept a little of the bad with the good!

Here are some common issues you may run into:

Component	For	Against
Performance computer chip	Increased power, realize benefits of other engine modifications.	May affect driveability and ability to pass emissions test.
Cat-back exhaust system	Slight gain in power, especially with other modifications. Louder (see also: Against).	Possible loss of ground clearance; Louder (see also: For).
Exhaust header	Slight gain in power, especially when combined with other modifications.	More exhaust noise; less ground clearance (with some designs); more possibility of exhaust leaks.
Power adders (nitrous oxide, turbocharging and supercharging)	Large power increase without tearing deeply into engine.	Greater chance of engine damage or short engine life if not properly set-up. Can cause you to fail an emissions inspection.
Performance camshaft	Significant power increase, especially when combined with other flow-improving modifications.	On bigger cams, rough idle, loss of low-rpm power; loss of engine vacuum (so power brakes may work poorly); Can cause you to fail an emissions inspection.
Nitrous oxide	Big power boost.	Power can come at the expense of engine components not up to the task.
Custom paint	Ultimate statement.	Expensive. At re-sale, will need to find someone else with exactly the same taste as you.
Body kit	Turns any common run-of-the-mill car into something unique and personal.	Can look cheap if paint and fit are not perfect.
Window tint	Help stop sun-fade of interior. More difficult for thief to see what goodies you have. Gives clean exterior look.	May or may not be 100% legal in your area.
Custom bucket seats	New look to the interior. Perfect final touch to other, more subtle, treatments. Can be more comfortable and provide better support over stock.	May not be compatible with standard seatbelt systems. Installation can be difficult if not designed specifically for your car.

A blast through the past

Where'd my Focus come from?

When you think of sport-compact cars and small-displacement four-cylinder engines, the name "Ford" does not immediately pop into most people's minds. But looking at the history of the Ford Motor Company, we see a wealth of success and experience with small cars and small engines.

Back in 1908, when Soichiro Honda was two years old, Henry Ford mass-produced his first lightweight, four-cylinder car. Yes, we're talking about the Model T. And in following years, Model T engines gained a reputation for being rugged and reliable. These tough little engines were the subject of many a hot-rod build-up. There were even overhead-cam conversions for these engines, and early Ford four-cylinder engines participated in all types of racing. Although Ford would continue to produce four-cylinder engines for the American market, the trend beginning in the 1920's was for bigger cars with larger, more powerful engines.

Fast-forward to the early 1970's. The USA was at the beginning of its "fuel crisis." Gone was the 29-cent-per-gallon gas that fueled the race for ever bigger cars and engines. American car companies reeled and were sent back to the drawing boards. But with its experience and worldwide connections, Ford was quickly able to field an efficient little car, the Pinto. While the first Pintos used engines designed in England and Germany, Ford quickly developed an American-built 2.3L overhead-cam four-cylinder engine. An advanced design for the time, this tough little engine, in updated form, would remain in production for another thirty years.

But Ford would not rest after the Pinto's success and developed its first front-wheel-drive car, the Escort, in 1981. The Escort was clearly an attempt to boost Ford to the forefront in economy cars and compete head-to-head with the imports that were steadily taking away sales. The Escort was in development for years, and Ford capitalized on the experience of its European divisions to make the best economy car possible. After some early teething problems, the all-new design, that Ford referred to as a "world car," became extremely successful. During its twenty-year production history, the Escort went through two design platforms, many changes and had several high-performance packages. Beginning in 1984, Escort GT's could be had with a turbocharged 1.6 liter engine that put out a solid 120 horsepower. This gave it more power than other competitive turbo cars of the time, and is still respectable by today's standards. By 1998 the Escort could make 130 horsepower with no turbocharger at all, thanks to a new 2.0 liter, 16-valve "Zetec" engine.

But the big news was coming in 2000. Ford had already been "testing" its true "World Car," the Focus, on European roads for over a year. The new Focus had it all – styling, first-rate engineering and, most importantly, performance. The excellent Zetec engine was carried over from the old Escort platform, giving it a better home in a more sporty and up-to-date chassis.

The result? Spectacular! Ford began selling Focuses by the hundreds of thousands and, after the usual initial bugs were worked out, the Focus provided the quality and reliability that Ford is famous for.

And the Focus stirred the tuner community's interest almost immediately. After all, here was a great-looking, up-to-date sport-compact that was well engineered, lightweight and, just to add novelty, American! Long-time Ford enthusiasts now joined with sport-compact tuners to build the ultimate Focus – and the race was on! Sport-compact shows throughout the country now featured wildly modified Focuses. Aftermarket companies began making all types of accessories for the new car, from body kits to engine parts. Then Focuses began appearing at dragstrips. Smirks and chuckles were silenced by clouds of tire smoke as Focuses scored regular wins against some of the toughest competition. This should have been no surprise, since Focus builders were backed by one of the most successful parts programs in the industry, Ford Racing!

The latest Focus is more refined than its predecessor, both in styling and performance. Ford has incorporated invaluable dragstrip experience from Ford Racing, which has culminated in the Focus SVT. The Zetec engine received a number of important upgrades, including a free-flowing exhaust system. The naturally aspirated SVT Zetec makes 170 horsepower, rocketing it to the highest levels of sport-compact performance. Here is a truly competent driver's car that produces more horsepower than the Honda Civic Si, for the same price. One might say Ford has regained its mastery of four-cylinder performance.

And many a Honda driver is getting nervous. . .

Aerodynamic/styling package, streamlined mirrors, trick taillights, de-badged decklid, custom paint - with the *right* combination of exterior modifications, you could have the coolest car on the block.

02

Body & exterior

Get it all *wrong*, however, and your precious project could end up looking more like some silly vehicle from a bad science fiction movie!

Body
and exterior

One way to avoid the latter outcome is to decide how you want to alter the appearance of your car and then do a *lot* of R & D: pore over catalogs and magazines, look at other guys' cars at shows, ask manufacturers the right questions *before* you buy anything.

Pay particularly close attention to "fit and finish." How well does a part - air dam, side skirt, rear valance, aero mirror, etc. - fit your car? Look for kits that fit well without requiring a lot of cutting, trimming or other alterations. How well finished is the kit? If it looks like #&*$ in gel coat, is it going to look any better painted? Be forewarned: body kits aren't all equal. Some fit the car they're designed for very well, some don't fit too well at all . . . even after considerable tinkering. Some are fiberglass, some are polyurethane (some of the newer kits are carbon fiber, but the prices of these kits will leave you gasping!).

The Ultimate Detail

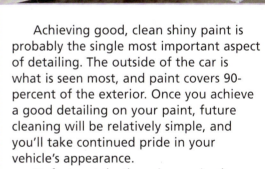

Step 1 Wash it

01 Start your detail with a good washing. Don't make the mistake of using the wrong kind of soap. Instead of strong household soaps, use dedicated carwashing soaps, which can be found at your local auto parts store

02 Use a pressure washer or hose nozzle to direct a really strong spray of water on the dirty areas such as the fenderwells, tires/wheels, bumpers, front spoiler and rocker panels. This will help dislodge any heavy deposits of road grime

03 It's important to wash and rinse a section of your car at a time, and in the shade, to prevent water spots from forming on your paint. Start with the roof and the windows, then the hood, grille and front fenders as the next section, followed by the rear and the sides. Do the tires and wheels last. The reason for doing a section at a time is to get to the rinse phase on each section before the suds and loosened dirt have a chance to dry onto the surface

Achieving good, clean shiny paint is probably the single most important aspect of detailing. The outside of the car is what is seen most, and paint covers 90-percent of the exterior. Once you achieve a good detailing on your paint, future cleaning will be relatively simple, and you'll take continued pride in your vehicle's appearance.

Unfortunately, there is no miracle cure for paint protection, just good protectants applied regularly with equal parts hard work and common sense.

04 Don't forget to wash the door jambs, interior edges of the trunk lid and the bottom of the hood, as they are difficult to clean later. Door jambs are best rinsed with a clean sponge and water, rather than with a hose which can get water spray on the interior

05 Proper wheel cleaner sprays can also aid in removing road grime and brake dust from rims

06 A car can be dried completely with a chamois, but there will be a lot of wrist-bending wringing-out when you get down to the last beads of water. Most pros use terrycloth towels for final drying. Such towels should be 100% cotton, and you should buy and set aside towels just for the drying phase of your detailing. Never use a towel for other aspects of detailing, such as waxing, polishing or wheel-cleaning, and expect to wash that towel out and use it some other time for car-drying

Step 2
Really clean the paint

Paint cleaning products come in varying degrees of abrasiveness, from rough compounds that are used only when machine-buffing a new, wet-sanded two-stage paint job, to polishing compounds that are good for getting off stubborn spots or treating really faded paint, to fine polishes and paint "cleaners." The condition of your paint surface determines how abrasive a treatment you need to achieve the shine we're looking for. The more abrasive the product, the more actual paint you will remove in the process of a clean finish, and you want to remove as little paint as possible. When restoring an old, faded paint job, it can be difficult not to polish through the paint and down to the metal! Even when polishing paint with a very fine abrasive, you are still putting scratches into the surface. In all cases, although the array of products you'll find at the store is overwhelming, you are well-served by very carefully reading the directions and cautions in the fine print on the back of the package as to the intended use of the product. The pros tell you to use the least abrasive product that seems to do the job for your application.

TIP:
Clearcoated paint requires the use of "clearcoat-safe" products when cleaning or polishing your vehicle's paint. You must read the product labels carefully to find out if they are safe for clearcoat finishes.

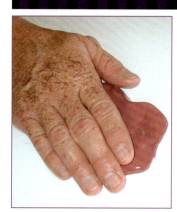

Our experienced detailer uses a polishing clay to clean small areas of the paint surface at one time. While working the clay, he keeps the area he's polishing lubricated with water

Step 3
Glazes and sealers for that brilliant shine

Sealers and glazes require buffing to achieve their effect, and then they must be waxed-over right away or the sun and atmosphere will start to dull them down immediately. So there is considerable elbow grease involved in using them, but if used properly the results may be the shiniest you've ever seen your ride!

When using sealers and glazes, it's vitally important that you read the directions on the product before use. Of course, like any detailing product, they should be used only on cool surfaces, preferably in the shade or indoors, but with plenty of lighting so you can really see where the minute scratches are and how well you're doing on evenly glossing the surface.

01 Most of the glazes and combination glaze/sealer products must be buffed off before they fully dry. They often contain resins that help them fill in swirl marks left by previous polishing or compounding. Using a back-and-forth motion with your cloth to apply the product, let dry only to a semi-haze . . .

02 . . . then buff with the same motion, not a circular motion. Buff until there is a high gloss. Some of the many glazes and sealers are very tough to buff out to a gloss if you let them dry fully, so do it in the shade and make sure your phone's answering machine is on when you start the project. You'll love the results of the glaze or glaze/sealer

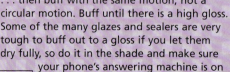

Tip
Use masking tape to protect rubber or plastic trim from glaze or wax residue

 Apply the wax of your choice following the manufacturer's directions, usually with a back-and-forth motion with a slightly-dampened cotton terry cloth and allowed to haze all over the car. The wax is buffed off by hand with clean terry cloth towels

TIP **Tip**
When waxing around areas such as chrome trim, fender emblems, antenna, etc., you should be cautious not to build up too much wax in the joints of mating surfaces. It may attract dirt later on and also can be hard to remove from detailed areas of trim without tedious work

Step 4
Wax it!

Wax is the final line of defense in your effort to shine and protect your car's paint, and its importance can't be overstated. All of the preparation work you've invested up to this point is lost if you don't wax the vehicle thoroughly and immediately. Everything we've suggested so far is aimed at getting a clean, smooth painted surface free of scratches, tar, bug stains or any other imperfections. Now you can use a good wax to protect all that effort. If necessary, use compressed air and a small brush to remove wax residue from small cracks or emblems

 After waxing, a vinyl dressing can be used to renew those faded trim pieces

 If the fenderwell undercoating flakes-off during a pressure wash, black spray paint can be used to touch-up the fenderwells

01 Clean the chip thoroughly with a special fiberglass-bristled brush

02 Use a standard touch-up applicator or a paper match to deposit the touch-up color into the cleaned-out chip, or . . .

03 . . . if a better match for your paint is available only in a spray can, aim the spray into the cup from the top of the can and then use that liquid paint for touch-ups with a paper match or toothpick for an applicator

Touch-up

Many minor scrapes and shallow scratches can be eliminated or reduced with nothing more than wax and polishes. Try this first before doing anything more drastic. If that doesn't work, then color it with a touch-up paint.

Most touch-up paint bottles have an applicator inside, or you can use the end of a paper match or a toothpick to apply it. The latter works best in applying only a tiny amount if necessary. The factory brush in the jar puts on way too much paint so that it usually makes a small chip end up looking a lot bigger. If you can't find the color you need for your car in a touch-up bottle, check your auto parts store in the spray-paint racks. There is a much wider selection of "original" touch-up paint colors in spray cans than in little bottles.

We illustrate here a method of repair using a "Chip Kit" which has all the supplies you need for a quality touch-up except the actual color to match your vehicle.

 Tip
Basic touch-up paint available from auto parts stores should be a close match to your car's paint, but due to the myriad colors and shades that come out each year, it can sometimes be difficult to find touch-up paint for more than a few years back. It is suggested that you buy a bottle or two when you buy your car and keep them in the glove box for future use.

04 Clear lacquer is applied in several coats after the original color paint has thoroughly dried, which usually takes several days

05 When the repair is built up to slightly above the surrounding paint, the area is sanded flat with several grades of ultra-fine sandpaper wrapped around a soft rubber sanding block

06 Very fine polishing compound is then used to blend the repair and sanded area into the rest of the paint

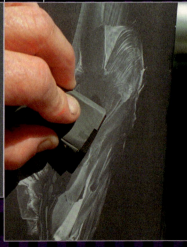

De-badging

You know that old saying about beauty being in the eye of the beholder? Well, you may not see things the same as Ford.

Just because Ford put a set of badges on your Focus doesn't mean that you're stuck with these eyesores. They're easy to remove. And your ride will look a whole lot cleaner without them.

01 To prevent any paint damage to the vehicle, construct a special tool using a scraper with duct tape placed on the end of the blade. Remove glued-on badges with a heat gun or hair dryer and your special tool. Try not to scrape off the paint underneath the badge

02 Be sure to move the tool slowly, allowing the heat to melt the glue before proceeding

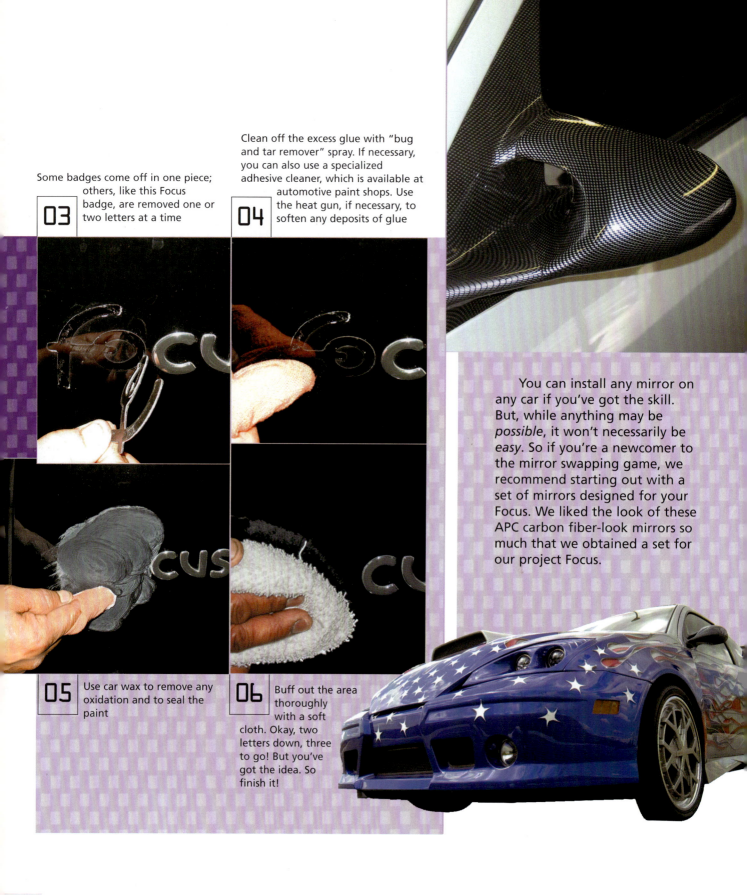

03 Some badges come off in one piece; others, like this Focus badge, are removed one or two letters at a time

04 Clean off the excess glue with "bug and tar remover" spray. If necessary, you can also use a specialized adhesive cleaner, which is available at automotive paint shops. Use the heat gun, if necessary, to soften any deposits of glue

05 Use car wax to remove any oxidation and to seal the paint

06 Buff out the area thoroughly with a soft cloth. Okay, two letters down, three to go! But you've got the idea. So finish it!

You can install any mirror on any car if you've got the skill. But, while anything may be *possible*, it won't necessarily be *easy*. So if you're a newcomer to the mirror swapping game, we recommend starting out with a set of mirrors designed for your Focus. We liked the look of these APC carbon fiber-look mirrors so much that we obtained a set for our project Focus.

Aftermarket mirrors

Installing custom mirrors

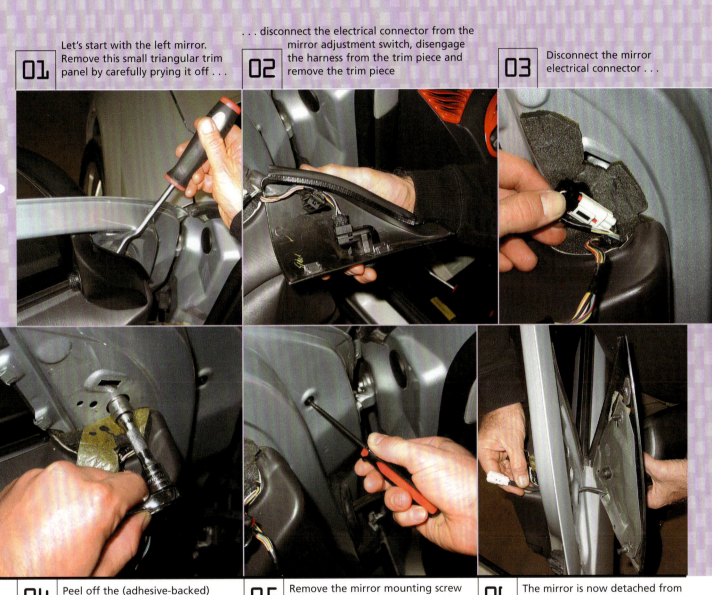

01 Let's start with the left mirror. Remove this small triangular trim panel by carefully prying it off . . .

02 . . . disconnect the electrical connector from the mirror adjustment switch, disengage the harness from the trim piece and remove the trim piece

03 Disconnect the mirror electrical connector . . .

04 Peel off the (adhesive-backed) foam insulation from the door, then unscrew the bolt

05 Remove the mirror mounting screw (it's a Torx) from the door

06 The mirror is now detached from the door. Carefully thread the electrical harness and connector through the door and remove the mirror assembly

07 Place the new mirror in position . . .

08 . . . loosely install the Torx mounting screw . . .

09 . . . loosely install the mirror mounting bolt, then make sure the mirror is correctly positioned and tighten the Torx mounting screw and the mirror mounting bolt securely

10 Carefully place the foam insulation in position again and push it firmly against the door to re-stick it . . .

11 . . . then reconnect these electrical connectors (even though you don't have power mirrors any more, you still want to prevent the connector halves from rattling around in there!)

12 Pop the trim panel in place and you're done with the left mirror. Now on to the right!

Custom headlights

The front end of a Focus is already pretty unique, but replacing those stock headlight housings will really set it off. If you want your car to stand out from the crowd, a straightforward headlight housing replacement is for you.

Installing custom headlights

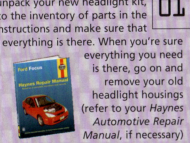

01 First, unpack your new headlight kit, refer to the inventory of parts in the instructions and make sure that everything is there. When you're sure everything you need is there, go on and remove your old headlight housings (refer to your *Haynes Automotive Repair Manual*, if necessary)

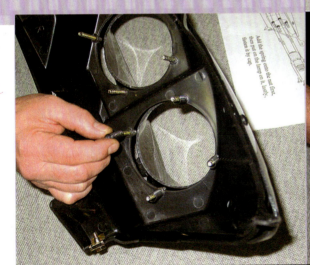

02 Some assembly required on the new headlight assembly: Install these springs on the studs . . .

03 . . . then install the headlights onto the studs; the headlights will be marked LOW (low beam) and HIGH (high beam). Make sure that you install the low-beam unit in the outer position and the high-beam unit at the inner position. And make sure that the both headlights are installed right side up (the top of each headlight should be marked TOP, or something similar)

04 Install the wing nuts and tighten them gradually and evenly (these mounting nuts are also the headlight adjustment nuts)

05 Once you've got both headlight units installed in the housing, plug in the electrical connectors . . .

06 . . . place the new headlight assembly in position and remove the three screws on top of the outer headlight housing. These three screws attach the outer part of the headlight housing to the inner part. Removing them separates the two parts, which gives you some wiggle room to get the housing assembly correctly aligned with the mounting bolt holes

07 Once the housing is correctly seated, install the two upper housing mounting bolts but don't tighten them yet . . .

08 . . . then re-install the three screws on top of the outer headlight housing, but don't tighten them yet either

09 From underneath the vehicle, install the lower headlight housing mounting bolt

10 And there it is! Now go do the other side! When you're done, adjust the headlights (see your *Haynes Focus manual*)

2-10

Aftermarket taillight assemblies

One of the hottest styling trends is installing clear, smoked or colored aftermarket taillight assemblies. Basically, all you have to do is remove the stock taillight assemblies and replace them with the aftermarket units of your choice. Don't forget that your running lights and brake lights must be red, your back-up lights clear and your turn signal lights amber. Your stock taillight lenses are already colored red, clear and amber for these lights, but you'll have to install the correct color bulbs if your aftermarket housings are clear.

Installing custom taillights

01 Carefully unpack your new taillights. Make sure that they're the style that you wanted and that they're undamaged. Now remove your stock taillight housings (refer to your *Haynes Automotive Repair Manual* for the procedure)

02 Give the bulb holders a counterclockwise twist and remove them from the old housing . . .

03 . . . and transfer them to the new one, giving them a clockwise turn to lock them in place. If equipped, push the wiring harness clips onto their posts on the new taillight

04 Flip the new taillight over, place it in position with its mounting tab aligned with the hole on the hatch side and its lower mounting stud aligned with the mounting hole in the vehicle body . . .

05 . . . then carefully push the new taillight into place. Make sure that the locator pin is fully seated (you should feel it "pop" into place) in its nylon clip. (We had to back out the locator pin on the new taillights a few turns in order to get it to engage the nylon clip.)

06 When you're satisfied that the locator pin is fully seated, install the mounting screw (shown) and the locknut (from the inside). That's it! Now go and do the other one

Before

Install a custom grille

Nothing sets off the front end of your Focus like a mesh grille. You lose that dull stock grille, which looks kinda like the thing at the bottom of a refrigerator, and you add function, too - it'll keep stuff like birds, plastic bags and other road trash off of your radiator, condenser and intercooler (well, if you're lucky enough to have one!) and out of your engine compartment. But admit it; the real reason you want a mesh grille is because it just looks right. Right? So get on with it . . .

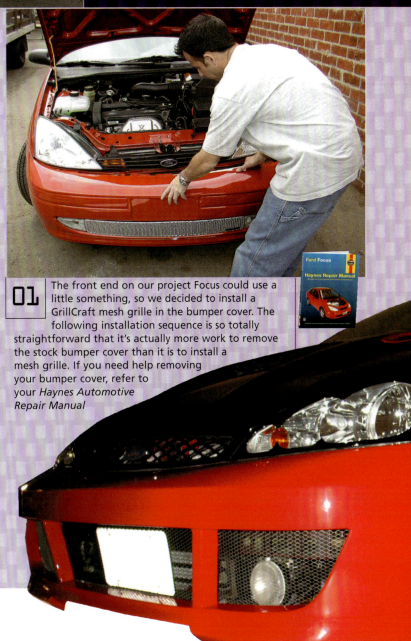

01 The front end on our project Focus could use a little something, so we decided to install a GrillCraft mesh grille in the bumper cover. The following installation sequence is so totally straightforward that it's actually more work to remove the stock bumper cover than it is to install a mesh grille. If you need help removing your bumper cover, refer to your *Haynes Automotive Repair Manual*

02 Install the mesh grille over the existing lower grille and hold it firmly in place

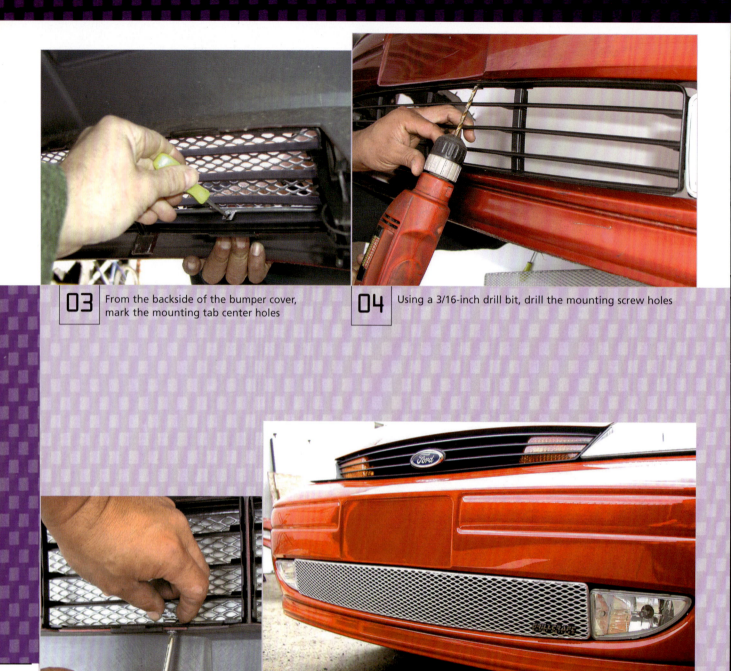

03 From the backside of the bumper cover, mark the mounting tab center holes

04 Using a 3/16-inch drill bit, drill the mounting screw holes

05 Attach the mesh grille using the mounting hardware supplied in the kit. That's it! Now go put the bumper cover back on!

06 Voila! Instant (almost) mesh grille!

No mesh grille kit available for your body kit?
Make your own!

A mesh grille kit is the way to go - IF the one you want is available for your car AND you can afford it. But sometimes you just can't find what you want, or don't have the coin to get it. If you find yourself in this predicament, don't be bummed! You have another option: Make your own mesh grille. You have several choices of styles, including the classic diamond shape and the "round hole" style. We selected the diamond shape because it just looks really cool on our Focus body kit's front bumper cover.

01 First, remove the bumper cover (see your Haynes Focus manual). Then place a piece of mesh slightly larger than the size of the hole you're going to mesh. Mark the area you need to mesh and mark the location of holes you're going to drill to secure the mesh to the bumper cover. Then cut out a piece of mesh about an inch larger all the way around so that you'll have plenty of room to screw down the mesh around the periphery of the hole. Don't try to cut this stuff with scissors; you're going to need a pair of metal cutting shears or tin snips

Making and installing a mesh grille

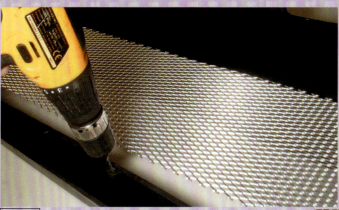

02 Push the mesh aside and drill some suitable mounting screw holes at the points you've marked. Be careful! You're not trying to drill a hole to China, you just want some little starter holes slightly smaller in diameter than the self-tapping screws you're going to use

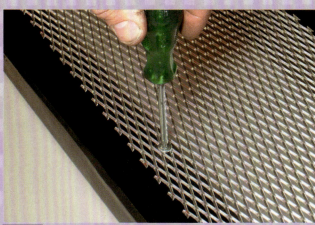

03 There are many ways to attach your new mesh grille to the body kit. Self-tapping screws are easy to install and very secure, but if they're too long they could end up protruding through the outside skin! This would not be good. You could also use a hot glue gun or fiberglass

04 After securing the mesh to the bumper cover, bend down the edges of the mesh. Use a shop rag to protect your fingers! All right then! Go ahead and do the two smaller side holes in the bumper cover the same way

Body & exterior

Aerodynamic body kits

Aside from a set of trick wheels or a custom paint job, an aerodynamic body kit is the biggest visual change you can make to your car.

The newest kits are easy to install because they already fit well, so little if any cutting or trimming is necessary. Some kits are fiberglass, but others use high-quality polyurethane.

Most modern aero body kits come unpainted. And if you decide to purchase a polyurethane kit, it will be a little more difficult to paint than a fiberglass kit because you have to add a flex agent to the base coat. Nevertheless, most automotive painters say that polyurethane requires far less prep work than fiberglass. But, hey, we don't want to let all this talk about painting bore you, or scare you off. If painting's not your thing, fine. Some kit manufacturers will pre-paint their kits (for an additional charge) so that they match most factory colors (but not custom paint).

If you decide to go with an unpainted kit, you will of course have to measure, mark, drill, cut, trim and install some parts, then remove them for prepping and painting, then install them again. Other parts are pre-cut and no drilling is necessary. They're attached to the vehicle surface with double-face tape - really, really strong double-face tape, so they must be painted before installation. Once you stick those pieces on the car, they ain't goin' nowhere!

Installing a new front bumper cover

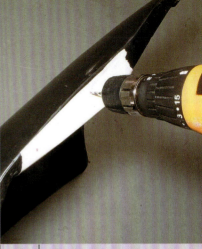

01 With the help of an assistant and the guidance of your Haynes Automotive Repair Manual, remove the bumper cover from the vehicle and store it in a safe place

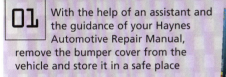

02 Still got your helper? Good! Place the new bumper cover in position and have your helper hold it in place while you mark the location of the side mounting holes. To make things easy, try to attach your new bumper cover using the original bumper cover mounting points

03 Once you've marked the locations of the side mounting holes, drill the holes

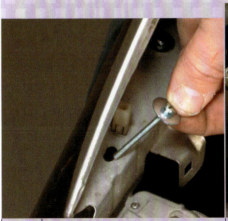

04 Attach the sides of the bumper cover to the fenders using suitable fasteners. Be patient! Tightening up the nuts on the underside of the bumper cover is a character builder!

05 Once the sides of the new bumper cover are secured, note whether the upper holes of the bumper cover are aligned with the stock bumper cover mounting holes. (The holes on our kit lined-up perfectly with the existing bumper holes.) If they don't line up, grab your drill again and make some new holes in the body

06 After we'd finished installing the front mounting bolts on our new bumper cover, we noted that the bottom of the cover had bowed up. So our clever mechanic devised a bracket that attached the underside of the new front bumper cover to the lower radiator support crossmember

07 Here's how our beefy bracket looks installed. The heavy-duty bracket pulled the bumper cover into place, stopped the bowing effect and offers additional support. Crude but effective!

08 Install a screw in each wheel housing and bumper cover installation is completed. Now that you've got the thing correctly fitted, all you have to do is remove it for painting (unless you want to mask the front end of the car!)

Tinting the back-up and rear fog lights

Since we weren't installing a complete new rear bumper cover, having opted instead for the ESP Design bumper cover extension/valance panel, we decided to have a little fun with the back-up and rear fog lights. We wanted to tint them with a special Folia Tec taillight tinting kit (there are other kits just as good, we just like this smoky shade!). Tinting is easy and takes very little time to do.

01 With the rear bumper cover already removed, simply pop out the two light units housed in the outer ends of the rear bumper cover

02 Give each light assembly a good cleaning with a suitable degreaser. (Yes, we actually used brake cleaner for this job! But you could also use contact cleaner, or one of those special degreasers they sell exclusively at paint and body supply shops. That's the best stuff, but you'll pay more for it.)

03 Once the light assembly is completely clean and degreased, use some Scotch-Brite to gently roughen up the surface. You do NOT want to deeply score the plastic lens; just lightly wipe over the lens itself.

04 Mask the area behind the light assembly to protect it from overspray

05 Next, read the instructions on your tinting can. Sometimes manufacturers state that you need to shake the can for a certain length of time to warm the paint material; others say that you should give the can a quick shake before spraying. Be sure to test the spray pattern to make sure that the nozzle is working correctly, then apply the first layer of paint. Allow each layer to dry thoroughly (read the instructions!) before applying the next coat. Repeat until the lights are tinted to the shade your want

Adding a valance panel to the rear bumper cover

Although there are a number of very sharp looking rear bumper covers available from the aftermarket, we wanted something unique for our Focus. So we obtained a rear bumper cover extension kit from ESP Design that gives our rear OEM bumper cover the aerodynamic look of an expensive new custom rear bumper cover, without the expense!

01 Removing the rear bumper cover is pretty much the same deal as the front. Refer to your Haynes Automotive Repair Manual if necessary.

Note: The rear bumper does not necessarily have to be removed in order to install an extension like the kit shown here. We removed it mainly to show you how to do it, secondly to tint the lights and thirdly to mesh the extension. Loosen the rear wheel lug nuts, jack up the rear of the vehicle and support it securely on jackstands (see the Jacking and towing section of your Haynes manual), then remove the rear wheels.

02 Some bumper cover extensions require a lot of cutting and hacking before they'll fit correctly to the underside of the bumper cover, but not ours - it fit perfectly on the existing bumper cover! It is mostly held in place with very strong adhesive and some screws in the wheel arches. Using a Scotch-Brite pad, rub down the mating surfaces of the factory bumper cover and the extension that will be glued together

03 Before applying any adhesive, place the extension in position and note the points of contact between the bumper and extension; this will save you wasting any valuable adhesive (you don't get a lot of extra glue with some kits). After you figure out where to put the glue, apply a bead of adhesive to the contact areas

04 You'll need some help for this step. Place the bumper cover extension in position and press it on firmly. While your helper holds it there, install some straps (we used motorcycle tie-downs) to hold the extension in place while the glue gets to work. Press firmly against the areas being glued together. It's gonna get messy, so clean off the excess adhesive with brake or contact cleaner. Once the adhesive has cured (check the instructions on the tube), you'll just have to get it painted to match

Side skirts

Side skirts were first used by Can Am and Formula One cars in the Seventies, which had a very low ride height, and flexible rubber side skirts that provided a seal against the track. Side skirts directed air passing over and around the car from getting underneath the vehicle, where it could upset or negate the downforce produced by the wing and/or the car's shape. Side skirts quickly spread to all kinds of motor racing, then eventually found their way to the street.

Aesthetically, side skirts "tie together" the front and rear bumper covers. They're also a clever way to visually "lower" your Focus, making it look like it's lower to the ground than it really is. But downforce? Get OUTTA here!

01 Drill a suitably sized hole in each of the mounting bolt bosses on the skirt (this one has three)

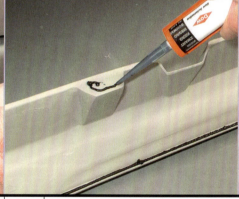

02 Place the skirt in its installed position on the car and, using the holes you made in the mounting bosses, mark the location of the holes you're going to drill in the body. Once that's done, go ahead and drill the holes

03 Wipe the mounting surfaces of the new side skirt and the rocker panel area of the vehicle with a good degreaser. It has to be REALLY clean!

04 Besides the lower mounting bolts and a retaining screw in each of the wheel housings, the skirt is held in place using a strong adhesive/sealant (supplied with some body kits; if your kit has no adhesive, get some silicone adhesive at an automotive retailer or a hardware store). Apply a bead of adhesive along the top edge and around the mounting holes and the skirt is ready to be installed. Get some help for the next step or it could turn into a very messy job. Place the skirt in position and, while your helper holds the skirt in place, install the three lower mounting bolts

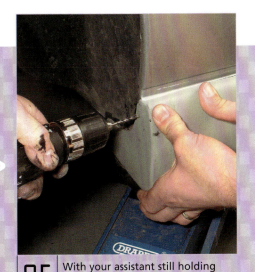

05 With your assistant still holding the skirt in place, drill a hole in each wheel housing, then install the screws

06 When you're satisfied with the results, tape down the skirt with very strong packing tape to hold it in place until the adhesive has dried. Most adhesives take at least 24 hours to become fully effective so the skirt will need the extra restraint while the glue agents do their thing. Besides, you're not going anywhere. You still need to install the other skirt!

Carbon fiber hoods

Carbon fiber is light, strong and expensive. Once used only on taxpayer-funded space shuttles and military aircraft, it eventually trickled down to Formula One and other racing series. Now it's widely available for the street, and it's still light, strong and expensive! There are carbon fiber hoods, mirrors, deck lids, wings, even body kits. None of these pieces are cheap, if they're made from the real stuff. Of course, the most obvious and distinctive carbon fiber upgrade you can make to your Focus is the hood. All it takes is money! The rest is easy.

01 Before removing your steel hood, get help. The hood isn't super heavy, but it's difficult to handle by yourself, and you might just want to reinstall it someday if you sell your car. Okay, first step is to disconnect the windshield washer fluid lines

02 If you think there's a good chance that you'll be installing the stock hood someday, mark the relationship of the hood hinge flange to the hood with a grease pencil or utility marker. Then, with your helper holding one side of the hood while you hold the other, remove the four bolts (two at each hinge) that attach the hood hinge flange to the hood (don't unbolt the hinges from your Focus - you're gonna need 'em). Carefully remove the old hood and set it down somewhere safe

03 Okay, let's install your new carbon fiber hood! Put some towels or shop rags at the rear corners of the hood to protect the paint, then guide the hood into position. Install the hood hinge bolts and tighten them just until they're snug, but not too tightly because you'll need to check the fit of the hood before final tightening of the hood hinge bolts

04 Carefully lower the carbon fiber hood and note whether the striker is correctly aligned with the latch mechanism. If the striker is off-center, the hood isn't correctly aligned. If the hood is slightly off-center, give it a little tweak to the left or right to move the hood on its hinges and center the striker in the latch, then look at the gaps between the fenders. Hood lined up with both fenders and gaps the same width? Okay, now you can tighten the hood hinge bolts!

05 One more adjustment you might have to make is the hood height, which is determined by the height of these two little rubber bump stops, which can be screwed in (lowers the hood) or up (raises the hood). Fool around with the bump stops until the hood is flush with the fenders. That's all there is to it! You're done!

Neon lighting

Inexpensive and easy to install, neon lighting is one of the easiest ways to give your ride the "show car" look. With the variety of kits available today, you can install neon to just about any part of your car you want. Just try to keep it away from surfaces that could scrape the ground or get submerged easily in puddles. And check your local laws to be sure you're not doing anything illegal.

When wiring, have a separate switch for your neon so it can be turned off when you don't "need" it, which will also help the components last longer.

03

Painting and graphics

Custom Painting

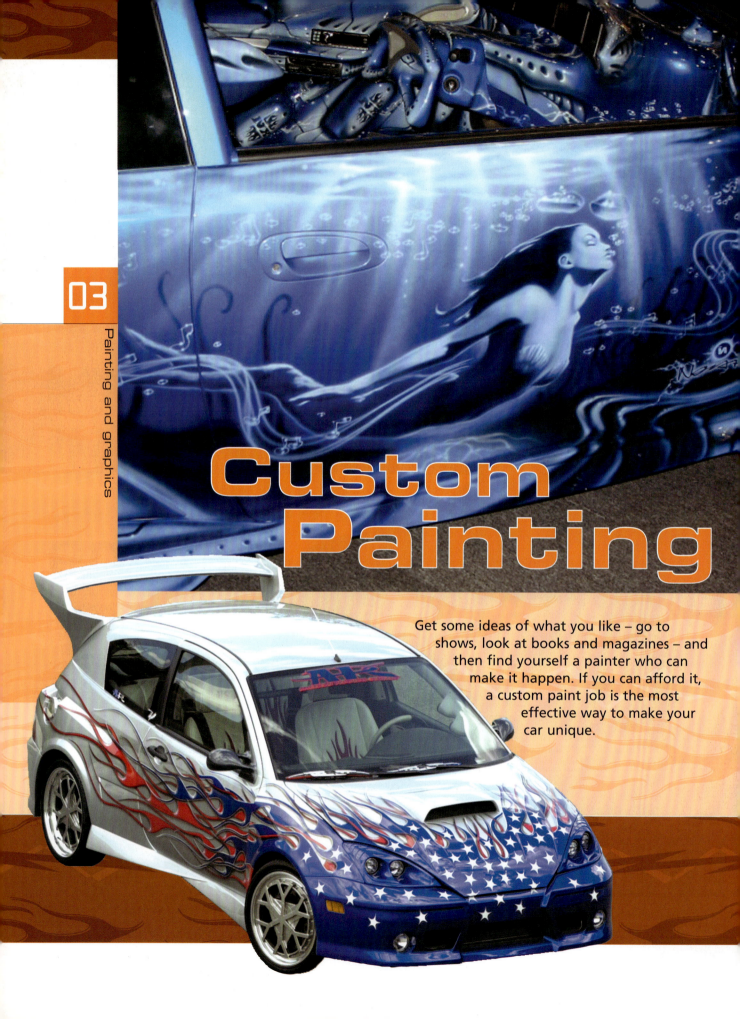

Get some ideas of what you like – go to shows, look at books and magazines – and then find yourself a painter who can make it happen. If you can afford it, a custom paint job is the most effective way to make your car unique.

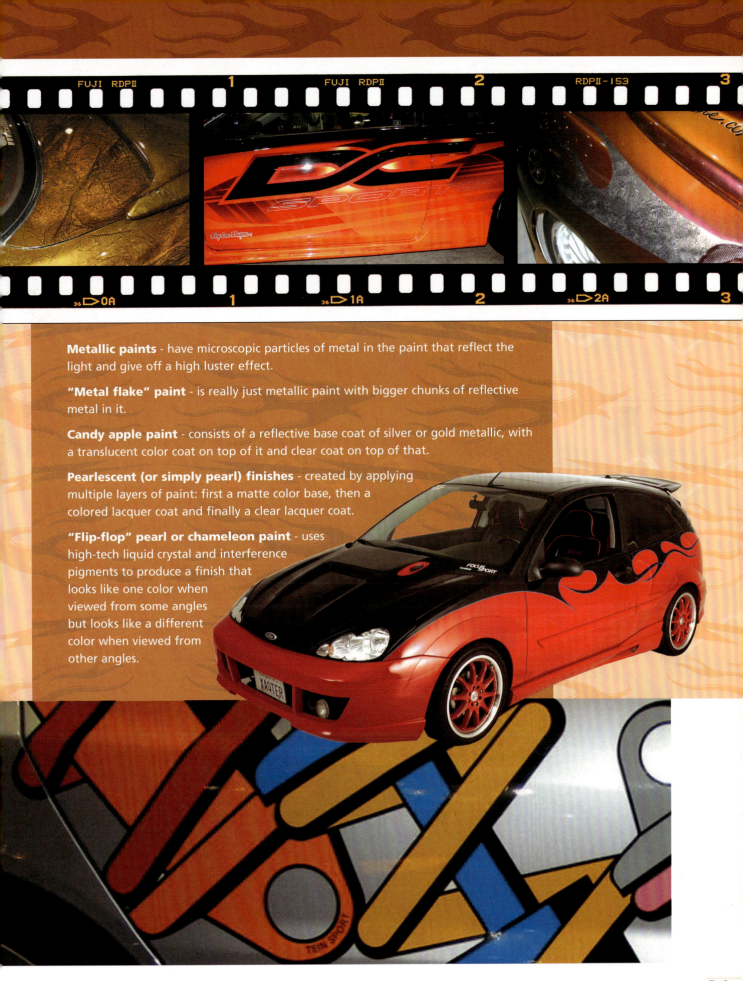

Metallic paints - have microscopic particles of metal in the paint that reflect the light and give off a high luster effect.

"Metal flake" paint - is really just metallic paint with bigger chunks of reflective metal in it.

Candy apple paint - consists of a reflective base coat of silver or gold metallic, with a translucent color coat on top of it and clear coat on top of that.

Pearlescent (or simply pearl) finishes - created by applying multiple layers of paint: first a matte color base, then a colored lacquer coat and finally a clear lacquer coat.

"Flip-flop" pearl or chameleon paint - uses high-tech liquid crystal and interference pigments to produce a finish that looks like one color when viewed from some angles but looks like a different color when viewed from other angles.

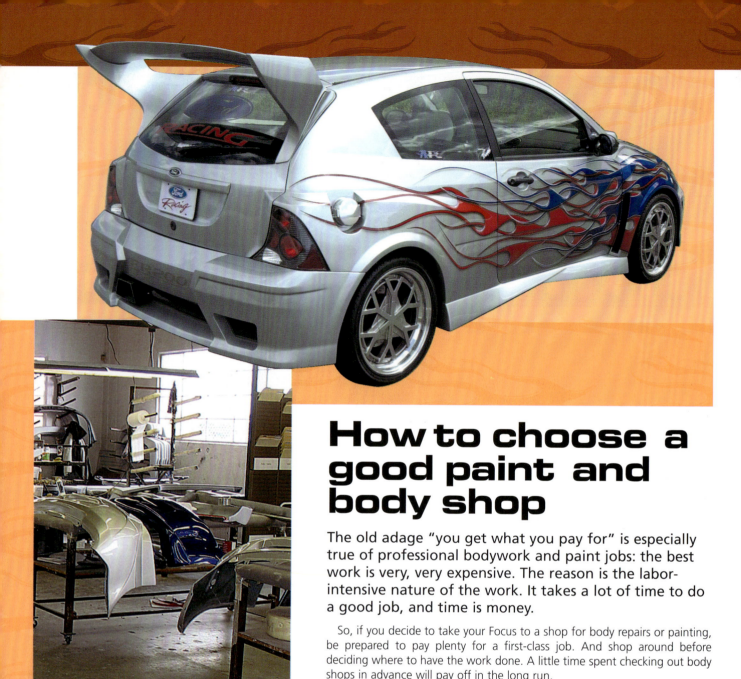

How to choose a good paint and body shop

The old adage "you get what you pay for" is especially true of professional bodywork and paint jobs: the best work is very, very expensive. The reason is the labor-intensive nature of the work. It takes a lot of time to do a good job, and time is money.

So, if you decide to take your Focus to a shop for body repairs or painting, be prepared to pay plenty for a first-class job. And shop around before deciding where to have the work done. A little time spent checking out body shops in advance will pay off in the long run.

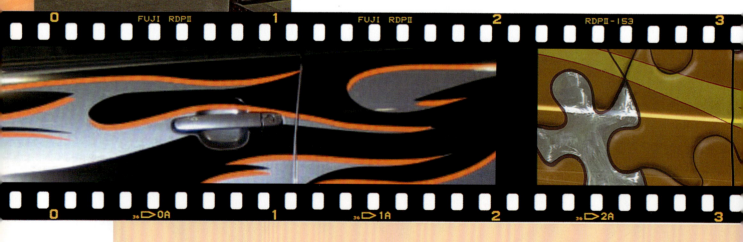

Don't let a shop's location scare you off. Most shops are located in industrial areas that can't be considered good neighborhoods. However, any good shop, regardless of its location, will have safe, secure storage areas - either indoors, outdoors or both - for customer's cars. If a shop doesn't have well-secured parking, keep looking.

As you drive up to a shop, note its general condition, how the surrounding area is maintained and the types of cars that are waiting for attention. If they all seem to be desirable collectors or luxury cars, you might have stumbled onto a top-notch shop. (You might also need to call your banker for a big loan!) Are completed vehicles stored indoors or outside? Are they covered or not? It might not be obvious at first glance, but details like these can make a difference between a great paint job and a good one, so ask the manager when you get a chance.

Ask the owner or manager to give you a little tour of the shop. Is it relatively neat and clean, or are there body parts and tools scattered all over the place? Is it well lit and roomy, or dark, dingy and cramped? Are the body repairmen and painters wearing neat new work clothes, or grungy old paint-smeared jeans and T-shirts? Is there plenty of room between the cars that are being worked on, or are they jammed together? Has any effort been made to protect the interiors of vehicles and the exterior parts that don't require work? What about new replacement parts and the old parts that have been removed from vehicles during repairs? Are they shoved into the interiors of the cars, or are they labeled and stored neatly in a separate area?

Look for a frame-straightening fixture, MIG, TIG and oxyacetylene welding equipment, and separate masking and painting booths.

Try to get a close look at some recently completed paint jobs. Note whether any dirt or lint is trapped in the paint. Look for runs and sags and see if the coverage is uniform and complete. Was everything carefully masked off? Or is there paint all over trim pieces? If it looks good, chances are that everything was done right.

If everything so far checks out, there's one more thing you should do: Ask the owner or manager if he would be willing to allow you to contact some recent customers so that you can ask them whether they're satisfied with the work done on their vehicles. If there's any hesitation at all, thank the person you're dealing with and leave. If the owner or manager is willing to put you in touch with recent customers, and if they're happy with the work done on their cars, you need look no farther.

Vinyl graphics

Custom vinyl graphics are a relatively inexpensive way to transform your Focus. A good vinyl graphics kit can be a lot wilder than a custom paint job for a lot less money.

But vinyl isn't perfect. For one thing, it's not that easy to install. Vinyl sorta goes on like a decal, but some vinyl graphics (like the kit shown on the following pages) are often much larger, and far more difficult to install, than a mere decal. And unlike paint, which can be quickly removed with reducer if you screw up, vinyl is pretty much toast if you commit a Major Mistake while applying it.

Installing custom vinyl graphics

01 First, round up the stuff you'll need for applying your vinyl graphics kit. We used a special stripping cleaner, isopropyl rubbing alcohol, a spray bottle with a slightly soapy water solution (mix a gallon of water with a single DROP of dishwasher soap), a heat gun, scissors, a gasket scraper (taped to protect the paint), masking tape, lint free shop towels and a squeegee (not shown)

02 Clean off the entire side of the vehicle with the special stripping cleaner

03 Using a few little pieces of masking tape to "hang" the graphic, figure out where you want to put it. Once you've determined the location and the orientation of the graphic, tape it to the car along the entire upper edge of the graphic pre-mask. This long piece of tape will serve as the "hinge" so that you can flip the graphic up and out of the way as necessary during the installation process

04 Okay, flip up the graphic and secure it to the window with a piece or two of tape, wipe off the area to be covered with alcohol, then spray the surface liberally with your slightly soapy water solution

05 Starting at the back (or the front, if you want), peel off the liner (the white backing sheet) from the graphic, working your way down in sections

06 As you peel off each section of the liner, spray the exposed back side of the vinyl graphic itself with liberal amounts of the semi-soapy water and apply the vinyl graphic to the car, spraying and peeling off the liner as you go

07 Once the liner is completely removed and the graphic is applied to the vehicle surface, work out the air and water bubbles with your hand first, keeping the graphic flat and preventing it from moving around. Start at the upper middle part of the graphic and work your way down and out toward the ends to prevent the graphic from bunching up

08 Next, work the graphic onto the surface with a squeegee. Again, work your way down and out from the upper middle part of the graphic

09 Starting at one end, carefully unpeel and remove the pre-mask. Lift the edge of the pre-mask off the graphic and slowly pull it back across itself at a 180-degree angle (pulling off the pre-mask at an angle of 90-degrees, i.e. straight up, might lift off the vinyl graphic with it). Pull with slow and steady pressure and be patient!

10 There are usually still some air and water bubbles trapped between the vinyl graphic and the vehicle surface. Carefully make small incisions with the point of a hobby knife. Do NOT make cuts with the blade of the knife. Just poke teensy little holes on the edge of each bubble and press out the air or water

11 There's one more thing you need to do: Using a straightedge and your knife, carefully cut the vinyl graphic wherever it crosses the gap between the doors and the body, and at the cover for the gas cap. Make your cut down the middle of the gap. That way, you'll leave a little extra on either side of the cut to wrap around the edge of the door or body sheetmetal

3-7

04 Interiors

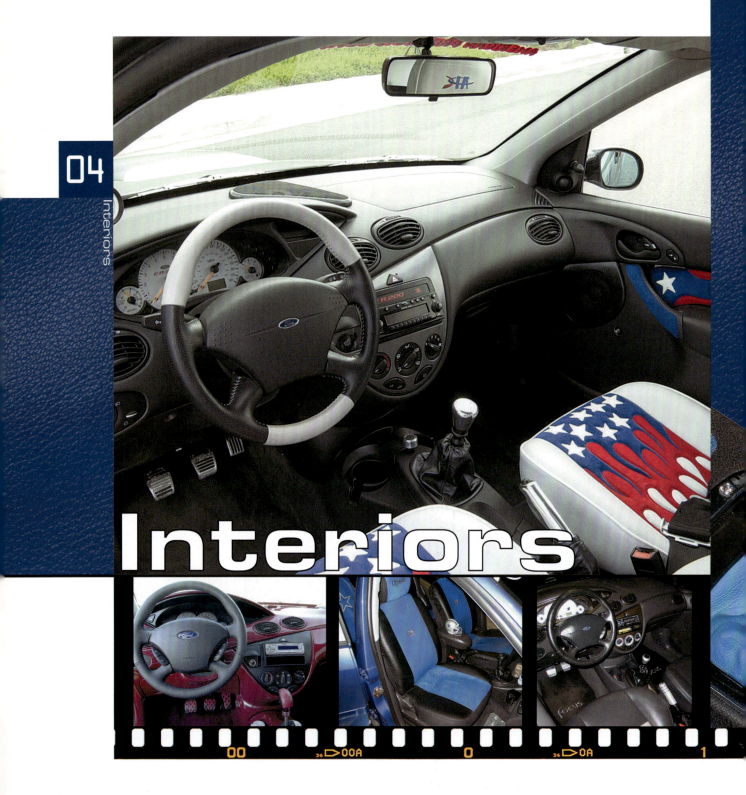

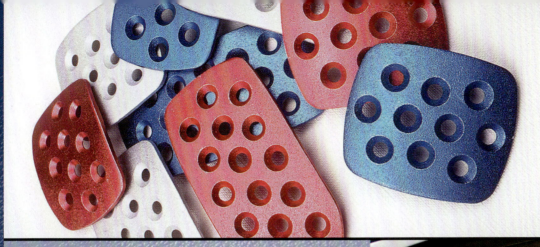

Are you sitting on an original equipment seat that bottomed out sometime long ago? Are you still wrapping your hands around a dull round blob of pebble-grain plastic posing as a steering wheel? Are you looking at a set of gauges that are hard to read at night and don't tell you much anyway? Are you surrounded by a dull expanse of faded and scuffed plastic trim panels on the dash, console and doors? Well, lovers of style and color, rejoice! It's easy, and inexpensive, to do away with all this dullness.

There has never been such a wide range of colorful, stylish and attractive products for interior upgrades as there is today. From steering wheels to racing seats, from control pedals to trim panels, the only limits to what you can do to your Focus interior are your budget and your creativity.

Installing a custom styling ring

01 Unpack your styling ring kit and then read the instructions

Custom styling rings for airbag-equipped steering wheels

Even though you can't legally replace an airbag-equipped steering wheel with a custom aftermarket steering wheel, you can upgrade the appearance of your stock wheel with a custom styling ring. Each ring is custom molded to fit over the stock steering wheel. Styling turn an ordinary airbag-equipped steering wheel into a stylish, elegant "new" steering wheel.

02 Clean off the steering wheel with a mild degreaser. Remove all dust, oil and silicone protectant

03 Peel off the protective strip covering the adhesive

04 Carefully position the styling ring over the steering wheel. Before pressing it onto the steering wheel, make sure that the spoke covers on the ring are perfectly aligned with the spokes on the steering wheel. Then press the styling ring onto the steering wheel. Work your way around the circumference of the wheel, pressing down firmly all the way around to make sure that the styling ring is firmly attached. Easy, huh?

Shift lever knobs

Think about it: Besides the steering wheel, there's no part of your Focus that you handle more than the shift lever knob. So why not upgrade it with something that looks and feels good. There are hundreds of aftermarket knobs in a riot of colors and materials that will fit your Focus shift lever. And one of them has your name on it!

Installing a shift lever knob

01 First, unpack your shift lever knob kit. We selected an anodized billet knob from APC for our Focus interior makeover. The kit includes the knob, set screws, an Allen key for tightening the setscrews, a set of bushings for different diameter shift levers, and a threaded trim bezel

02 To remove the stock shift lever knob from the shift lever simply unscrew it

03 Select a bushing with the same inside diameter as the outside diameter of the shift lever then push the bushing firmly down onto the top of the shift lever until it's fully seated

04 Place the trim bezel on the shift lever

05 Install the set screws in the shift lever knob, but make sure that you don't screw them in so far that they protrude through the inside wall of the knob, or the knob won't fit over the bushing

| 06 | Install the knob on the shift lever and tighten the setscrews. If there is no spring-loaded REVERSE lockout, your Focus uses an iB5 transaxle; go ahead and tighten the setscrews securely, screw the trim bezel onto the knob and you're done! If your Focus uses a spring-loaded lockout for REVERSE, it has an MTX75 transaxle; tighten the setscrews just enough to hold the knob in place, then go to the next step |

| 07 | Now comes the tricky part for you MTX75 owners: To be able to put the shift lever into the REVERSE position on one of these models, the shift lever knob must be installed high enough on the shift lever to allow the spring-loaded lockout to be pulled up, so screw on the trim bezel . . . |

If you can't pull the gear release up far enough to release the lever to put it into REVERSE, unscrew the trim bezel, loosen the setscrews, carefully raise the shift knob a little bit, retighten the setscrews, install the bezel and try again. Repeat this process until you can put the shift lever into REVERSE, but don't raise the knob any more than absolutely necessary, because those setscrews must be gripping the shift lever!

| 08 | . . . then try to pull up on the spring-loaded REVERSE gear release. If you can pull it up far enough to unlock the shift lever so that it can go into REVERSE, the knob height is correct. Unscrew the bezel, tighten the setscrews securely and reinstall the bezel |

| 09 | |

Installing a custom handle and dust boot on the parking brake lever

| 05 | We had to remove the old boot from the console and separate the boot from its bezel |

| 06 | We stretched the new boot over the bezel and drilled a few holes around the perimeter . . . |

Custom pedals

Race replica pedal covers

Have you ever noticed the accelerator, brake and clutch pedal pads on a race car? They're not ugly rubber-covered steel pads like street car pedals. Instead, they're aluminum, with holes drilled in them for lightness. In other words, no frills - stripped for action!

But until recently, when the rubber pads on your Focus pedals wore out, you simply replaced them with new rubber pads because that was your only option. Now you can pick a set of race replica pedals from literally hundreds of styles: brushed or polished aluminum, color-anodized, with or without lightening holes, with or without color-coordinated inserts. Some of the latest high-end pedals are even available in carbon fiber. The inserts (the small projections attached to the upper face of the pedal, to provide traction on the slippery surface of the pedal) are nylon, plastic, rubber or carbon fiber. Combined with other racy interior upgrades, a set of pedal pads gives your Focus a race car look.

Selecting a new set of pedal covers

When selecting a set of race replica pedal covers for your Focus, pay close attention to a couple of things. First, the new pedal covers will have three or four mounting bolt holes in them. When installing the new pedal covers, you'll be using these mounting holes to attach the new covers to the old steel pedal footplates. But you'll also have to drill mounting holes in the old footplates, and those holes must be aligned with the mounting holes in the new covers. So it's a good idea to either take the dimensions of your old steel pedal footplates with you when you go to buy new pedal covers, or to be able to take the new covers out to the parking lot, place them in position on your pedals and "eyeball" the dimensions. If the new pedal covers have mounting holes sitting over nothing but thin air when you position them over the old rubber pedal covers, think seriously about a different set of aftermarket pedal covers! The stock pedal footplates must be large enough so that you'll be able to drill mounting holes in them without having to relocate any of the new pedal covers. Relocating the pedal covers could cause clearance problems between the pedals. And, more importantly, it could be dangerous to offset the pedals because you might accidentally depress the wrong pedal at the wrong time.

Inexpensive, "easy-to-install" pedal covers, which slip over the pedal pads and clamp into place, are widely available. Just be aware that, even when installed properly, they have the potential of slipping and interfering with another pedal, which could cause an accident.

Installing a set of race replica pedal covers

01 Remove the old rubber covers from the accelerator, brake, and clutch pedals

02 An easy way to center the brake and clutch pedals covers on the factory pedals is to draw a line down the middle of the stock pedals . . .

03 . . . so you can center this line in relation to the center holes of the new pedal covers before you make your marks for drilling the mounting holes

04 When you've got your mounting bolt holes correctly positioned, use a punch to make some indentations for the drill bit . . .

05 . . . then drill the holes in the pedals

06 When you're satisfied that the pedal covers are correctly positioned, tighten the Allen bolts securely. We can't overstress the importance of making sure the pedal cover bolts are tight. It's a good idea to check the tightness of the bolts a few weeks after installing them

07 And that's it! One racy looking set of pedals!

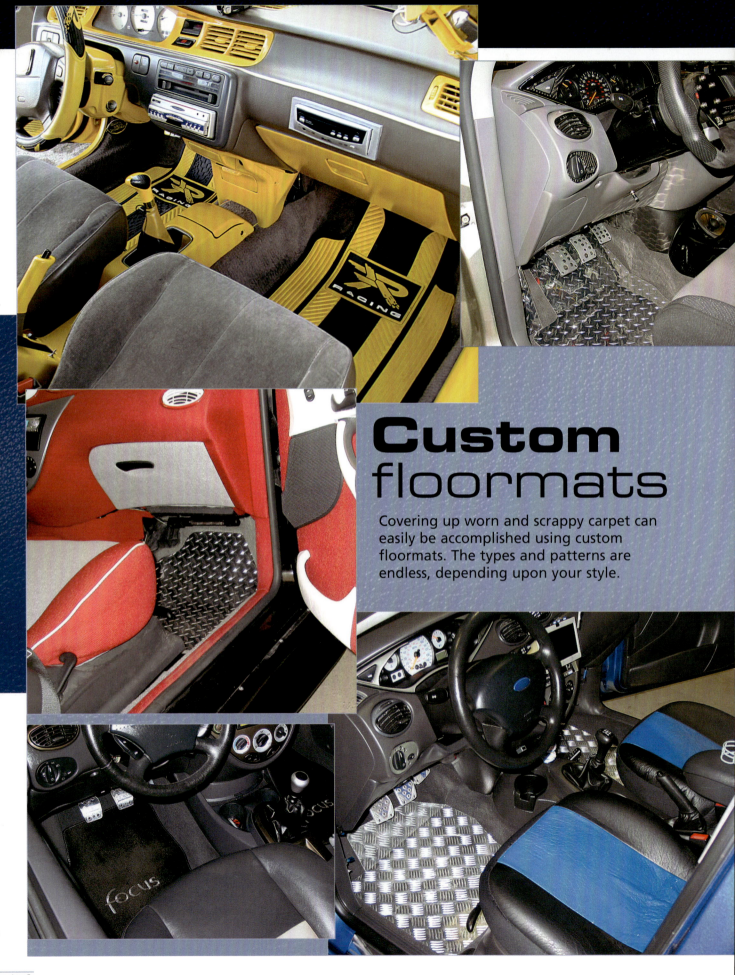

Custom
floormats

Covering up worn and scrappy carpet can easily be accomplished using custom floormats. The types and patterns are endless, depending upon your style.

Installing neon lighting under the dash

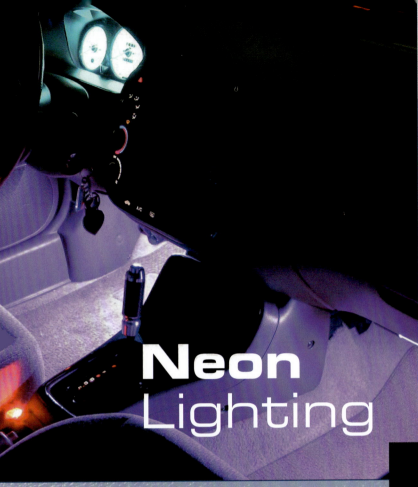

Neon Lighting

Glowin' in the dark could not be easier or cheaper. So flip the switch and get with it

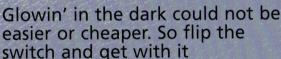

01 Most kits include an enclosed neon light assembly, an electrical lead, an adapter to plug into the cigarette lighter and the instructions. We decided to install a pair of purple neon lights under the dash, one for the driver and one for the front-seat passenger, and a blue neon light in the backseat footwell area

02 Position the neon light assembly under the dash and try to find a place that will provide you with a solid installation. We picked this spot because it was flat and we could drill into it without hitting anything vital

03 Mark the location of the mounting screw holes

04 Drill the mounting screw holes with a drill bit a little bit smaller in diameter than the screws you're going to use

05 Install the mounting screws and tighten them securely, but don't really crank on them. This is a plastic accessory being mounted on a plastic dash, and we all know what happens to plastic when you overtighten it!

06 Either unplug your cigarette lighter or, if you have an electrical accessory receptacle, use that

07 Plug in the electrical adapter. That's all there is to it for the passenger side. Installing the other neon light for the driver is virtually identical to this procedure, except for one thing . . .

08 . . . if you install two (or more) neon lights, you can't plug them all into the cigarette light (or an accessory outlet). Of course, you could splice the two electrical leads into one adapter. But at that point you might as well splice the two (or more) leads through a switch you can flip on and off

⚠ Warning !
The use of neon lighting may not be legal in all areas. Check it out first. Also remember that driving at night with a brightly-lit interior makes it even harder to see out. Neons are best used at shows or in the parking lot.

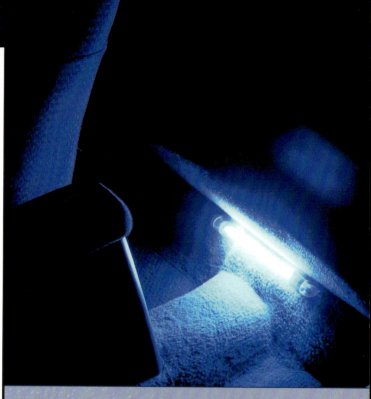

Installing neon lighting in the rear footwell

01 Position the neon light assembly where you want it. We selected the area right below the center of the back seat because we figured one light would provide plenty of illumination for both rear footwells

02 Using a laundry marker, mark the positions of the mounting screws

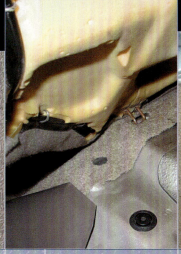

03 We needed to figure out where to route the electrical lead for the neon light. We decided that behind and under the carpet was our best choice. So we removed the rear seat cushion bolts (see your Haynes manual for the specific rear seat removal procedure for your car) . . .

04 . . . then we lifted up the rear edge of the back seat cushion . . .

05 . . . unhooked the forward edge and removed the rear seat cushion

06 Then we removed this push fastener, peeled back the carpet and routed the neon light's electrical lead down and forward . . .

07 . . . and then pulled it through the hole in the carpet for the parking brake lever (center console removed). From here, we could route it forward, under the console, to the cigarette lighter or the switch we installed earlier for the front

08 With the electrical wiring routed under the carpet, place the carpet back in position and install the push fastener

09 Using the marks you made in Step 2, drill holes through the carpet and the body for the neon light mounting screws

10 Install the light, secure it with the mounting screws, reinstall the seat and you're done!

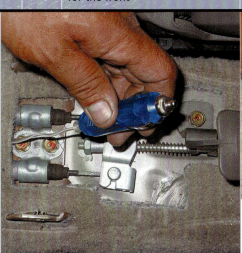
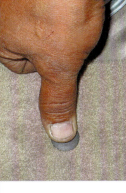

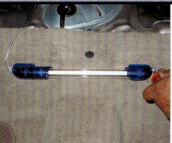

Interior trim

Add a little color to your interior

Automotive exteriors come in lots of nice colors, but most stock interiors are still mainly black, gray, or beige. Boring!

But it doesn't have to be that way. There are three ways to add a little (or a lot of) color to your interior: paint it, "film" it or re-cover it with new trim pieces. Interior trim film is a new high-tech product that you can buy in sheets and cut to fit various trim pieces on the dash, the center console and the doors. Film is UV and heat resistant and it's available in a variety of finishes - simulated woodgrain, carbon fiber, etc. - and colors. Trim covers are also available in a similarly wide range of finishes and colors.

Painting trim

01 First, remove the trim panels you want to paint. We decided to start with the inside trim panels for the outside mirrors (refer to your Haynes manual if you're unfamiliar with how to remove these pieces)

02 Give each piece a really good scrubbing with a Scotch-Brite pad to rough it up (paint adheres better to a rougher surface). When you're done, give it another soap and water bath, then dry it off

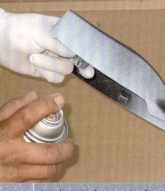

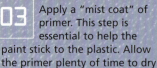

03 Apply a "mist coat" of primer. This step is essential to help the paint stick to the plastic. Allow the primer plenty of time to dry

04 Apply the first topcoat very "dusty," which means you must spray from a little further away than normal, letting the paint fall onto the job, rather than blasting it on using the full force of the aerosol spray propellant. Some colors need several coats before they look right. Allow time for each one to dry (several minutes) before applying the next coat

05 When you're done with both sides, re-install the mirror trim pieces and voilà! Check out the color match with our billet stainless trim panel covers!

Applying film

01 First, remove the trim panel(s) you want to film. (refer to your *Haynes manual* for help). Using a suitable degreaser, clean up the surface you want to film. If you're hoping to film a heavily grained finish, be aware that the grain will show through thin film, and the film won't fully stick to a heavily grained surface either

02 Cut the film to the approximate size and carefully warm up the film and the panel itself with a heat gun. Peel off the backing sheet, and make SURE that the film stays as flat as possible. Also make sure that, when you pick up the film, you don't allow it to stick to itself!

03 Carefully apply the film. If you're installing a patterned film (like the carbon-fiber-look film shown here), make very sure that you apply the film with the pattern aligned horizontally and vertically. Starting at one edge, work across to minimize air bubbles and creases. If you get a bad crease, unpeel the film a bit and try again. Don't try to shift the position of the film once you've begun to apply it; the adhesive is far too sticky

Before trimming your filmed panel, work out the air bubbles with a soft cloth. Then make sure the film is sticking well by going over it firmly with the edge of a plastic credit card **04**

Trimming the panel can be tricky. It's easier to trim the more complicated edges after heating up the film with a hairdryer or heat gun. But don't overdo it! Also, make sure that the hobby knife you're using is SHARP. A blunt knife will ripple the film, and might even tear it **05**

To get the film to wrap neatly around a curved edge, make several slits almost up to the edge, then heat up the area you're working on, wrap each sliver of film over the edge and stick it on firmly. If you heat the film sufficiently, it wraps around and keeps its shape. Without the heat, the film might spring back, ruining all your hard work **06**

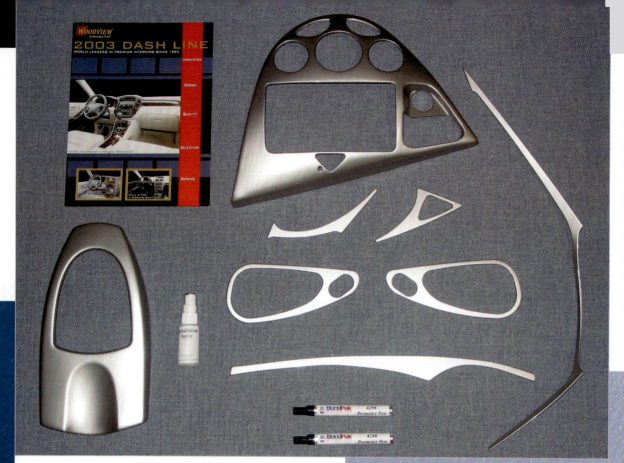

Installing a custom trim panel kit

Unpack your new trim panel set and make sure that everything is there. And make sure that you have the right kit for your make and model! To keep the adhesive side of each individual trim piece dust-free, don't detach it from the backing paper until you're ready to install it. (And it's not a bad idea to wash your hands thoroughly to remove any oil so that you don't put fingerprints on anything!)

01 Here's the basic process. Let's start with the trim pieces surrounding the inside door handles. First, make sure that your new trim piece is a good fit. If you see any irregularities, now is the time to cut them off, clean them up or send back the kit!

02 Wipe off all oil dirt silicone protectant, etc. with rubbing alcohol

| 03 | Now apply the adhesion promoter to the surface of the trim piece. Some kits include a pen-type promoter like this one, which is convenient, neat and precise. Other kits give you some promoter in a small container, which you apply with a cotton swab | 04 | Peel off the adhesive backing from the new trim panel . . . | 05 | . . . and press the panel into place | 06 | On curved surfaces like this one, use a heat gun to warm up the new trim panel while you apply pressure. The heat makes the panel more pliable so it can adhere more closely to the curved surface |

| 07 | Work your way around the interior, putting the remaining pieces in place |

Gauge face upgrade

White, colored, even glow-in-the-dark . . . changing out your stock black gauge faces will really add a custom touch to your dash

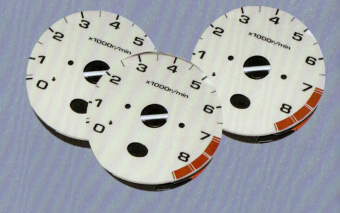

01 Unpack your luminescent gauge face kit and make sure that everything is there. Then read through the instructions carefully before proceeding. Make sure that you understand the procedure. If you're nervous about any phase of this project, then ask a more experienced friend, preferably someone who's already installed luminescent gauge faces, to help you. Or farm it out to a professional installer

02 First thing to do is to remove the instrument cluster. Refer to your Haynes Automotive Repair Manual for this procedure if you can't figure it out

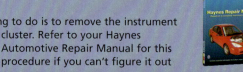

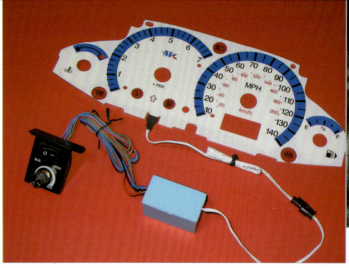

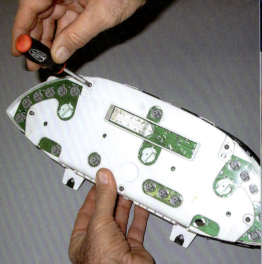

03 Okay, here we go! Some disassembly of the cluster is necessary in order to remove the odometer-reset button, which must be removed before you can install the new luminescent gauge face. First, remove the Torx screws retaining this white plastic piece from the backside of the cluster . . .

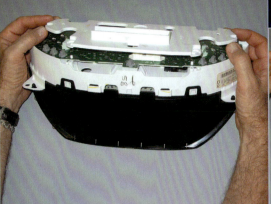

04 . . . remove the white plastic piece . . .

05 . . . then remove the circuit board

06 Disengage and release the locking tabs along the lower edge of the cluster assembly . . .

07 . . . and along the upper edge, then separate the cluster bezel (the clear plastic lens and black plastic housing) from the cluster (the gauge assembly)

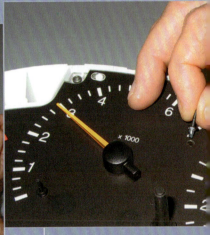

08 Once the cluster and the cluster bezel have been separated, carefully pull off all three of those little black plastic needle "stop" posts (two on the tachometer, one on the speedometer)

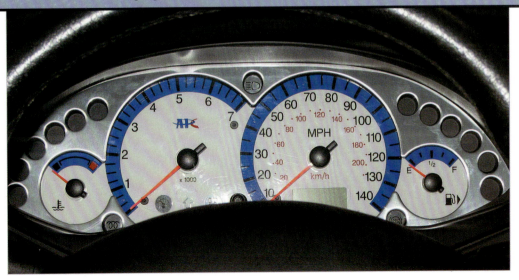

Just make sure you get the right kit for your car, and don't start stripping anything until you're sure it's the right one. Look carefully at every detail. Applications for replacement faces should be very specific for model and model year. This is one mod that is not ONE SIZE FITS ALL.

09 Remove the three screws that retain the gauge face to the cluster assembly . . .

10 . . . and remove the gauge face from the cluster assembly

11 To remove the odometer reset button from the gauge face, squeeze these two little tabs together with a pair of needle nose pliers, pulling on the button at the same time

15 Carefully place the cluster bezel in position over the instrument cluster and push down, making sure the locking tabs snap firmly onto their corresponding lugs. Okay, the cluster is finished. Place it in position and loosely install the four cluster mounting bolts. Now let's move on to the fun stuff: the switch, the converter box and the wiring

16 We picked the underside of the lower steering column shroud as the location for the switch. Go ahead and remove the shroud (see your Haynes Automotive Repair Manual), then mark the location of the screw holes . . .

17 . . . and drill them using the proper size bit

12 Carefully install the new gauge face onto the cluster by working the needles through the holes. Start with the tip of each needle and work your way down to the needle hub. Luckily, the new gauge face is flexible so you can bend it a little to work the needle hubs through the holes. Once the new gauge face is in position, install the odometer-reset button and the needle stop posts

13 Okay, that takes care of the new gauge face. Before we install the cluster in the trim bezel, we're going to install a brushed aluminum trim piece inside the cluster. First, wipe off the surface on which the trim piece will be installed with an alcohol pad (which should be included with your kit)

14 Test fit the trim before you peel off the protective film and the adhesive backing. Work the trim piece into the cluster bezel and make sure that it fits. On our trim a couple of spots around the edge of the trim were hitting the inside walls of the bezel, so we had to file the trim down a little bit. When we were happy with the fit, we removed the protective film and the adhesive backing and stuck the trim on the bezel

18 Now drill a hole big enough to fit the switch through

19 Install the switch and tighten the mounting screws securely

20 Flip the steering column shroud over and place the converter box in this location (the lower right corner of the shroud) - not somewhere else, where it might hit something on the steering column when the shroud is installed. We mounted ours with a piece of double-stick tape and a cable tie, which required drilling two holes

21 Connect the electrical leads for the converter box and the luminescent gauge face, then install the lower steering column shroud

4-19

22 Tighten the four instrument cluster mounting bolts securely, then install the trim bezel and the upper steering column shroud

23 Look for a fuse that's hot only when the parking lights are turned on, then remove the fuse

24 Using your test light again, probe both contacts of the fuse terminal to find the "downstream" or "fused" side of the terminal. You don't want the contact that's hot all the time; you want the contact that DOESN'T turn on the test light. Install a fuse tap on the end of the fuse that will correspond with the contact that did not turn the test light on, then reinstall the fuse

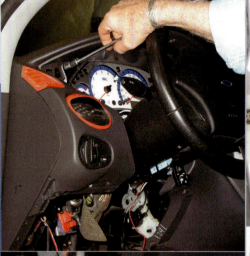

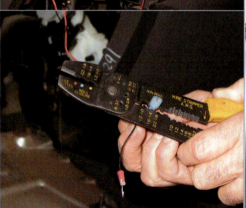

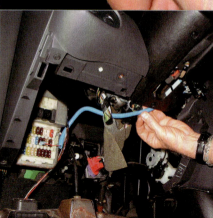

25 Strip off a 1/4-inch of insulation from the ground wire and crimp on a hook terminal, then strip of a 1/4-inch of insulation from the power wire and crimp on a female spade connector

26 Connect the female spade terminal to your fuse tap on the headlight fuse, then find a good grounding point for your ground wire (a bolt under the dash with good metal-to-metal contact)

27 Using split loom, cover the wiring and tuck it safely out of the way and out of sight, then install the knee bolster. That's it. You're done! Now go turn off the lights in the shop, turn on the lights and check out your new gauge faces!

Installing aftermarket gauges

Installing pillar pod gauges

01 Get your pillar pod and dummy it up exactly where you want to put it. Make sure it's a good fit before proceeding. Then, drill a hole at each corner of the pod as shown

02 Place the pod in position on the pillar and mark the locations of the four holes you're going to drill. Make sure the holes aren't going to be too close to the edges of the pillar

03 Insert the gauges into the pillar pod, place the pod in position on the pillar, then rotate the gauges so the "OIL" and "VOLTS" on the gauge faces are horizontal and parallel to each other

04 Remove the pillar pod and clamp the gauges into place with the clamps provided by the manufacturer, then connect the wires. Note how we spliced the two illumination bulb wires and the two ground wires together

05 Route the wires and the oil line for the oil pressure gauge through the gap between the end of the dash and the A-pillar, then install the pillar pod/gauge assembly on the pillar and attach it with the four mounting screws. Don't overtighten the screws or you'll strip out the holes. When you're done with this phase, hide the wires between the pod and the dash with some split loom tubing

Bucket seats

If you're doing a complete makeover of the interior, sooner or later you'll have to decide what to do with the old seats.

If you've already discovered how difficult it is to brace yourself during hard cornering in a seat with no support, you're probably ready to replace the front seats with something a little sportier. And if your tired old La-Z-Boys just happen to be bottomed out, broken, stained or threadbare, then the decision's made! Make a pair of aftermarket bucket seats the centerpiece of your new interior. Nothing says serious go-fast car like a pair of racing buckets (with racing harnesses, of course). Bucket seats are available in a wide variety of colors and styles and features: Recliners and non-recliners; fabric, leather, vinyl, velour, suede (and pseudo-suede!); integral headrests and separate headrests; heated and non-heated; lumbar support and no lumbar support; and . . . well, you get the idea. Somewhere out there are two front seats with your name on them! But before you go seat shopping, here are some things to think about.

First, keep in mind that the seat mounting brackets and the "runners" (the rails on which the seat assembly slides back and forth) are proprietary. In other words, they're part of the original seat assembly, and a new seat won't necessarily fit without some modification. So make sure that there is a mounting kit for the seats you want so that you'll be able to install them in your car. If there isn't, then either think about some other seats, or be prepared to do some fabrication.

Original equipment seats may not be very supportive, but they are adjustable fore-and-aft and they can recline, i.e. the seatbacks can be tilted to a number of positions. Most aftermarket sport buckets are also adjustable fore-and-aft, and most of them are recliners. Installing recliners in a coupe will allow you to keep using the rear seats, if that's important. But if you're planning to install real racing seats, be forewarned: real racing seats are not recliners. If you decide to install non-recliners, the seatback angle will be fixed, so make sure that the seating position is comfortable for you. Also, consider that non-recliners will make access to the rear seats in a coupe difficult, if not impossible. If you're also planning to install racing harnesses with the new seats, you will render the rear seats essentially inaccessible. So plan on turning your car into a two-seater if you decide to go this way.

Are you going to install a racing harness with each new seat? If so, make sure that the new seats have holes in the headrest for the shoulder straps. Racing harnesses can be installed in cars with seats that don't have these holes, but they won't look as integrated, or as racy. The good news is that you don't have to use (non-reclining) racing buckets to get those shoulder-strap holes. Many recliners are also equipped with these holes as well.

Removing the old front seats

> **Warning!**
> If your Focus is equipped with side-impact airbags or seat belt pre-tensioners, refer to your Haynes manual and disable the supplemental restraint (airbag) system. It is essential that you disable this system before proceeding

01 Remove the seat mounting bracket bolts at the front . . .

02 . . . and at the rear. The seat is now detached from the floorpan

03 Lift up the front of the seat and disconnect the electrical connector from the underside of the seat . . .

04 . . . then carefully remove the seat. Okay! That was easy! Now go remove the passenger seat!

01 First, attach the ends of the seat adjustment release bar to the slider rails

02 Install the support brackets (the straps with holes in them) and the slider rails to the seat bottom and tighten the bolts in accordance with the seat manufacturer's specifications

03 To attach the mounting brackets to the slider rails, install an Allen bolt through the end of each mounting bracket and the slider and tighten the nut securely with a ratchet and socket while holding the bolt with an Allen wrench. When both mounting brackets are attached to both slider rails, tighten the four fasteners to the torque specified by the seat manufacturer

Installing racing bucket seats

If you're going to buy a pair of racing buckets, make sure that the manufacturer has the right brackets to fit the stock mounting bolts holes in the floorpan. These holes are a government-specified diameter and thread pitch, and they're located at spots in the pan that are specially reinforced to withstand the tremendous forces involved in the event of a collision. You don't even want to think about making new holes in the floorpan for seat bolts. So make sure that your kit includes brackets designed to fit your Focus. If you get the right mounting kit, installing a bucket seat can be as easy as one-two-three . . .

04 To attach the seat belts to the new floor mounting brackets, place the lower end of the seat belt in position, install the bolt, then tighten the bolt to the torque specified by the seat manufacturer

05 All right then, you're in the home stretch now! Just two more jobs to do: First, bolt the seat mounting bracket to the floorpan (there are four bolts - one at each corner) and tighten the bolts to the torque specified by the seat manufacturer

06 Finally, bolt the slider rail mounting brackets to the seat mounting bracket. When all four bolts are installed, tighten them to the torque specified by the seat manufacturer

07 And there they are. Kind of tough to get in and out of, but once you are in, you won't be doing any sliding around!

Window tinting

First, pick your day, and your working area, pretty carefully - on a windy day, there'll be more dust in the air, and it'll be a nightmare trying to stop the film flapping and folding onto itself while you're working. Applying window tint is best done on a warm day (or in a warm garage), because the adhesive will begin to dry sooner. Don't try tinting when it's starting to get dark!

01 Step one is to get the window that will be tinted extra clean inside and out. Do not use glass cleaners or any other product using ammonia or vinegar, since both of these ingredients will react with the film tint or its adhesive and create a mess. It is also worth cleaning the working area around the windows because it is too easy for stray dirt to attach itself to the film tint. On door windows, lower them down partially to clean all of the top edge then close them tight to fit the film tint

02 Before you even unroll the film tint, beware - handle it carefully! If you crease it, you won't get the creases out. Unroll the film tint and cut it roughly to the size of the window

The downside to tinting is that it will severely try your patience. If you're not a patient sort of person, this is one job which may well wind you up - you have been warned. Saying that, if you're calm and careful, and you follow the instructions to the letter, you could surprise yourself.

In brief, the process for tinting is to lay the film on the outside of the glass first, and cut it exactly to size. The protective layer is peeled off to expose the adhesive side, the film is transferred to the inside of the car (tricky) and then squeegeed into place (also tricky). All this must be done with scrupulous cleanliness, as any muck will ruin the effect (difficult if you're working outside). The other problem which won't surprise you is that getting rid of air bubbles and creases can take time. A long time. This is another test of patience, because if, as the instructions say, you've used plenty of spray, it will take a while to dry out and stick.

Legal eagle: *The laws on window tinting* vary from region to region and are sometimes confusing at best. Do some research on the film you intend to use and then contact your local authorities. Otherwise, install the tint with the understanding you could get stopped and have to strip it off.

03 Spray the outside of the window with a weak, soapy water solution. Some film tint kits will provide a cleaning solution for your vehicle, but if not, use a little bit of dish soap in a spray bottle and apply the solution sparingly to the windows

04 Lay the sheet of tint onto the glass, with the protective film (liner) nearest you. Check this by applying a small piece of sticky tape to the backside and front side of the corners of the tint and film and carefully separate them. It will then become obvious which side is the sticky side of the tint and which side is the protective film

05 Spray the outside of the film with soapy water

Use a squeegee to get rid of the air bubbles and place the tint on the outside of the window glass.

06 Remember, the protective film (liner) will be facing out

Use a sharp knife and be sure not to damage your paint or window rubber. Trim the perimeter of the tint to the outside of the window. On some rear glass and tailgate glass there are wide black bands on the edges of the glass. Cut your tint to the inside of these bands or the tint will not fit when it is transferred inside. Use

07 a straight edge when cutting the tint

Now go inside the vehicle and prepare the glass for receiving the tint. Tape some plastic sheet to the door trim panel to prevent water damage when the tint is applied. It is a good idea to remove the door trim panel first, before going ahead with the job. Spray the inside of the glass with a soapy solution. Remember, no ammonia products

08 such as glass cleaner or vinegar

Working on the outside of the glass, it is time to separate the tint from the protective film. Use two pieces of tape to

09 pull apart the film at the corner

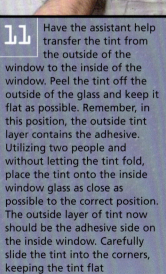

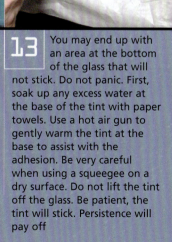

10 As the film comes apart, spray more solution on the tinted piece underneath to help it come apart cleanly. Try not to lift the tint off the glass too much as this will cause excess creasing. Have the assistant stabilize the tint to prevent any movement while the protective film is being removed from the tint layer

11 Have the assistant help transfer the tint from the outside of the window to the inside of the window. Peel the tint off the outside of the glass and keep it flat as possible. Remember, in this position, the outside tint layer contains the adhesive. Utilizing two people and without letting the tint fold, place the tint onto the inside window glass as close as possible to the correct position. The outside layer of tint now should be the adhesive side on the inside window. Carefully slide the tint into the corners, keeping the tint flat

12 Spray the tint with soapy water and carefully squeegee it into place, working from the top to the bottom. It is easier to use the squeegee blade separated from the handle to access the corner spots

13 You may end up with an area at the bottom of the glass that will not stick. Do not panic. First, soak up any excess water at the base of the tint with paper towels. Use a hot air gun to gently warm the tint at the base to assist with the adhesion. Be very careful when using a squeegee on a dry surface. Do not lift the tint off the glass. Be patient, the tint will stick. Persistence will pay off

Wheels & tires

05

If there is one crucial first customizing step in the process of making your economy compact into a sport compact, it's the tires and wheels, and of those two it's 90% the wheels. The right wheels can set your car apart in a way that makes it noticeable from two blocks away, even if the rest of the car remains unimpressively stock.

Wheel and brake size brings up questions of fit and appearance - this wheel has plenty of clearance around the brakes, but makes the brake look a bit small

Most street wheels are cast aluminum, with this example being a one-piece design

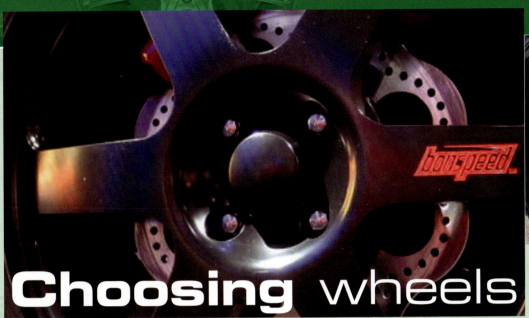

Choosing wheels

Two-piece wheels are very popular because they are less expensive than the one-piece, though they may weigh a little more - weight is a factor mostly for racing

Custom wheels are mostly purchased to attract attention, but they do have practical considerations. A wider wheel allows you to install wider tires for better traction. A set of custom aluminum wheels may be lighter than your stock steel wheels and thus reduce the amount of unsprung weight in the chassis, which leads to improved handling. However, the weight savings of the aluminum may be negated if you go much bigger than stock in the new wheels. A 20-inch-diameter aluminum "show" wheel might actually weigh more than your stock 16-inch-diameter wheels!

Have in mind the style of wheel you like long before you enter the tire/wheel store. Once you're in the store, the vast display of wheel choices can make the final selection more headache than fun. Observe the other Focuses you see and look at the wheels/tires closely. If you can find the owner of the car, ask him if he had any problems with the tires/rims he chose. Once you spend the money to get new rolling stock, you'll want to be happy with them for a long time to come.

Also look at cars like yours in magazines and see which wheels appeal to you, as well as scoping out the wheel advertisements. When you see wheels you like on a Focus like yours, read further and see what other modifications may have been made to accommodate those tires/wheels. Was the car lowered, and did it have custom wheelwells or an aftermarket body kit? Those custom body alterations may have given the clearance needed for those tires/wheels. Getting a picture of how complicated the simple act of choosing wheels and tires can get?

Two-piece wheels have the center section joined to the aluminum rim, either by fasteners or by welding

Plan ahead

If you're the type who is mostly interested in extracting total performance from the engine, while leaving your Focus pretty much stock as far as suspension and the body are concerned, you can just add tires and wheels that fit your car just the way it is. However, if you think that later on you'll lower your car with some aftermarket springs, you must consider the clearance between the tires and the fenderwell lip. It's cool to have a tire/wheel combo that fills the wheelwell, but not so cool to drive around with the outside edges of your tires worn away from rubbing the body.

A tire/wheel package that fits your car now may create interference when the car is lowered an inch or two. You can tell the guys whose tire-to-body fit is less than optimal. They're the ones who enter the driveway of your favorite hangout really slow, and with the car at an extreme angle to the driveway to keep from having rubber meet paint.

If you are thinking of adding flared fenders or a custom body kit to your car at some point, this will have a major impact on your wheel/tire choice. If you want really wide tires and big rims, you almost have to run something aftermarket in terms of bodywear just to clear the tires. On the other hand, you may have a good amount invested in the custom wheels/tires on your car currently and they may look too small if you add a body kit. Figure the cost of new rims and rubber into your budget if you are going to utilize a wide-body kit on your car.

Rim width on custom wheels is measured at the inside of the wheel lips, not the outside as you might have thought

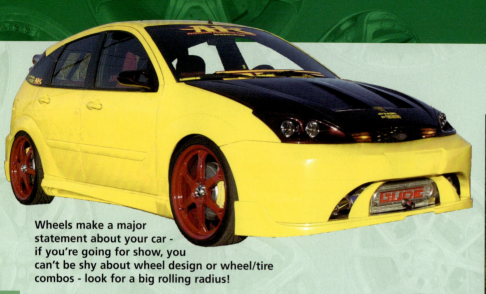

Wheels make a major statement about your car - if you're going for show, you can't be shy about wheel design or wheel/tire combos - look for a big rolling radius!

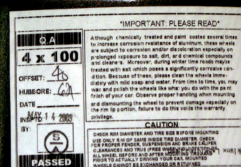

This wheel sticker's information includes: wheel offset, 40mm; bolt pattern, 4 bolts on a 100 mm circle; hub bore; and date of manufacture

Rolling radius

Rolling radius is the distance from the center of the wheel to the edge of the tire's tread. Most of us simply look at the tire/wheel diameter, rather than the radius. Without having to find the exact center of the wheel, you can measure the diameter with a tape measure simply by going from the ground to the top of the tire. Since tires vary in height as well as width, just knowing that a car has 18-inch wheels doesn't tell you how tall the rolling radius is, but a handy pocket tape measure will.

The existing final drive ratio in your transaxle is affected by the rolling radius of the tire/wheel size you choose. With a taller rolling radius at the tire/wheel, the effect is to make the final drive even more of a "cruising" ratio, which is not what you and I want for acceleration.

If you don't want to increase the rolling radius but still make the upgrade to taller wheels, you'll have to choose a tire that is shorter in section height. If your stock tire was a 75-series or 60-series, for instance, changing to a wider 55 or 50-series tire on your one-inch bigger new wheels may give you the same rolling radius as your stock tires and wheels, without taking away any gearing effect on performance. If you go up one inch in rim diameter, decrease the tire profile one size. A step up in wheel and tire size from a typical stock combo of the factory wheels with 185/65R-14 tires to 15-inch aftermarket wheels and a

Some wheels are marked only with decals rather than cast-in numbers - this sticker indicates the wheel load rating and the maximum recommended tire diameter (rolling radius)

fatter-but-shorter 205/50 hunk of rubber will give you better handling and traction, but not be so tall in rolling radius as to ruin your acceleration.

Confused? Well, a 205/55x15 tire (that's a 15-inch wheel, obviously) has a rolling radius of 607mm. Upgrading to a 17-inch wheel means fitting a 215/40x17 rubber with a nearly-identical rolling radius of 606mm. Stay within ten percent of your original height and you should be okay. Rely on wheel/tire combos that you know have worked successfully on other Focuses, plus listen to the advice of a good tire and wheel shop. They've probably seen all the right and wrong combos!

Wheel weight

If there were no other considerations when buying wheels, we'd always go with the lightest available. Lighter wheels are easier to accelerate or slow down and they are easier on your suspension. Unsprung weight is that weight in your car that has to bounce up and down over the road with your tires. If you have a big set of tires they can improve road grip on corners, but the heavy unsprung weight is like asking the suspension to work harder. Unfortunately, really light wheels are expensive! Most of us are more concerned with the outward appearance of the wheels than their performance benefit at the track, so we pick the wheel for our Focus that has the best compromise between the factors of weight, looks, and price. The cast wheels commonly available are much less expensive than the forged variety.

If you're really serious, use a common bathroom scale to weigh the wheels - the lighter the better for handling

Wheel offset

There's much more to the measurement of a wheel than its diameter. The amount of wheel offset is critical to fitment problems with the body and even the brakes. That flat, machined section on the back of a wheel that fits directly against your brake disc, drum or hub is the area we're concerned with. If that section is in the exact center of the wheel (in a side or end plane), the wheel is considered to have no offset. If the mounting plane is closer to the back of the wheel than the front of the wheel, that wheel will stick further out from the car than a "centered" wheel.

All wheels for FWD cars have a considerable offset to the inside of the car, meaning that flat mounting surface is closer to the outside of the wheel. Just how much offset is what matters. A wheel with a certain offset or wheel-center design may not clear the brake calipers or some other suspension parts on your car. A wheel with too much offset to the outside may cause the tire to interfere with the fenderwell lip. The correct wheel for you lies somewhere in between.

There are no universal standards for marking wheels with their offset dimensions. Some have the offset cast into the back of the wheel, some have a sticker on the rim, and some are unmarked. However, the offset of a wheel is easily measured with a ruler and straightedge. Lay the wheel down on a flat surface and measure the height of the rim. If the measurement is 200 mm, then the center of the wheel is at 100 mm. Place

This car has a large wheel and equally oversize brake setup - braking and appearance are equally satisfied

Wheel offset has perhaps the most influence on tire/wheel fit - the off-car wheel here has all the offset possible to tuck the wheel in, while the on-car rear wheel has less offset and more rim showing - to fit a customized body, front and rear wheels may need to be different

To measure a wheel's offset, lay a straightedge across the back of the rim, then measure from there down to the wheel's mounting surface - this measurement compared to the wheel's theoretical center gives you offset

Depending on the shape of the wheel's center, interference with a big caliper may come at the side, not just the outer edge - this one just clears

If you're planning for competition, you'll need the widest tire you can fit, which requires a wheel with lots of offset to tuck the wide tires inside the wheel

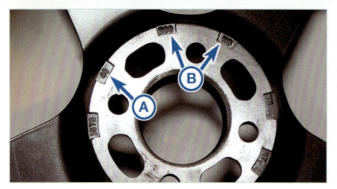

On most wheels, some important information is marked on the backside of the wheel - this one-piece wheel indicates the offset is 40 MM (A), and that the maximum load rating (per wheel) is 500 KG (B), or 1100 pounds (more than enough for any Focus!)

a straightedge across the wheel on the backside and measure from that edge down to the flat mounting surface of the wheel where the bolt pattern is. Let's say that measurement is 140 mm. This measurement is also called the backspacing, and it means the wheel has the mounting surface 40 mm further to the front of the wheel than the theoretical center. The offset is 40 mm.

For purposes of checking a wheel's offset, measuring the width of rim as described works fine, since we're just looking for the centerline measurement. However, when wheel sizes are described, the width measurement that is used is only the space between the tire mounting beads, not the lip-to-lip measurement. A wheel that is nominally 17x8 would be eight inches between the two tire beads. Measuring between the outside edges would be too confusing, since wheel designs vary greatly in the amount of lip width.

Used wheels

If you tend to swap parts around between your car and your circle of buddies, or you contemplate buying a set of wheels at a swap meet, there are a number of things to check. Bring a tape measure that has both inch and metric measurements. We've just outlined above the simple measurements that determine rim width and offset.

Another thing to worry about when selecting wheels is the bolt pattern. Most cars have four or five nuts or bolts holding each wheel to its hub. Different manufacturers use different bolt patterns for their wheels, so, just because two wheels have the same number of lug nuts doesn't mean they will interchange. Make absolutely sure the bolt pattern is correct before you throw down your hard-earned cash!

Take one of your existing Focus wheels off and make a paper or cardboard template of the bolt pattern. Place the paper over the machined mounting surface at the back of the wheel and rub a lead pencil over the paper until the location and dimensions of the bolt holes are clearly outlined. Keep this paper with you when you are wheel shopping and you won't get stuck with a set of Mitsubishi wheels that won't fit your car. Hold the paper behind the wheel you're examining and all the holes should line up with the bolt holes in the wheels.

Some wheels are made with two different bolt patterns to fit different model cars - this makes them less expensive for the manufacturer, and a good deal for the consumer

Stay centered

How a wheel is located on a particular vehicle's hub can vary. A "hub-centric" wheel is one that is located on the car's hub by a closely-machined opening in the center of the wheel that is matched to that car's hub diameter. Some wheels are "lug-centric" which means that the center of the wheel doesn't locate perfectly over the hub, but the lug nuts and lug nut holes are tapered to locate the wheel that way.

Your original Focus wheels are machined at the center to locate properly on your hubs. Most good aftermarket wheels are also machined to fit a specific application. There are some companies, however, that make most of their wheels in a basic, one-size-fits-all dimension, and rely on inserts that go behind the wheel to achieve the correct fit to center the wheel on various makes of car. Enthusiasts prefer to have a wheel that is located precisely on their specific car.

Many wheels have plastic or metal rings inserted on the backside to make an exact hub-fit on a particular application, always make sure the ring is in place before mounting a wheel

Extra-long studs protruding through "racing" lug nuts not only gets you through tech inspection, they also look racing-cool on the street

Wheel lug nuts/studs

To protect the finish on your wheels during removal/installation, use special plastic liners over your lug socket or wrap the socket with electrical tape

The relationship between the wheel studs in your car's hubs and the lug nuts used to secure the wheels on those studs is a critical safety consideration. Where most enthusiasts get themselves in trouble in this area is by using wheel spacers to achieve a look or fit by increasing the offset of a wheel. Spacers go between the wheel and the hub to move the wheel outboard a little.

If you use the same lug nuts that you had originally before the spacers were added, the amount of wheel stud that is threaded into the lug nuts is reduced by the thickness of the spacer.

Most wheel experts dislike wheel spacers, preferring their customers buy the right wheel for the job in the first place. There is no hard-and-fast rule about how many threads need to be engaged between the stud and the lug nut, but you should never reduce this dimension beyond the amount engineered by your car's manufacturer. If your car had 5/8-inch of threads into the lug nuts, stick with that dimension. To achieve this with spacers or some wheels that have thicker mounting areas (like built-in spacers), you should remove the hubs from the car and replace the studs with longer ones.

To protect your investment in cool tires and wheels, you'll want to use a set of locking lug nuts - use one per wheel, and don't lose the special "key" adapter required to remove them

A word to the wise. If you ever contemplate running your car at a track, whether a test run at the dragstrip or weekly assaults on the slalom course, the track officials will examine your lug nuts, specifically to see that enough threads are engaged. On many typical aftermarket wheels, the lug nuts have closed ends. The officials will ask you to remove one of your closed-end lug nuts to check for thread engagement. On wheels with open-end lug nuts, they can see how much thread engagement there is. It varies with the sanctioning body, but most organizations like to see a certain amount of stud threads sticking out beyond the end of an open-end lug nut.

Lug nuts are important! The two types are tapered (left) and straight (right) - the tapered ones (like stock lugs) center the wheel over the hub, while the straight ones don't exactly, so the wheel must have an exact center at the hub

Lug nuts may look alike, but pay attention to their markings or you could strip your wheel studs - this one is marked "12x1.5", which means it's for a 12 mm stud with 1.5 thread pitch

Lug nuts also come either open at the ends or closed - if you ever plan on competing, the inspectors will want you to have the open type, so they can check how much stud is engaged with the lug

Some wheels have a thicker mounting flange than your stock wheels - using a thicker wheel or wheel spacers means you should have longer studs pressed into your hubs for full thread engagement

If you are planning on lowering your Focus, make sure the wheels/tires you purchase aren't going to be too tall or too wide for the body in the lowered stance

Choosing tires

Along with the custom wheels, tires are an important part of both the looks and performance of your Focus. If you want the ultimate look, you'll get the tires and wheels that are as close as possible to looking like a rubber band has been wrapped around a 21-inch wheel. Not only is this nice to look at, it's race-inspired. In hard cornering, stock tires do not stay centered on the wheel. They "roll under," so that the tread area actually moves away from the center of the wheel. When this happens, the tread distorts, the tire "breaks away" and starts sliding. On low-profile tires, roll-under is almost non-existent, so the tire can keep a consistent tread "patch" on the road. Tires designed for long tread life are usually made from a very hard rubber compound and therefore will last a very long time. But hard-compound tires don't stick to the road as well. So most high-performance low-profile tires are made from softer, stickier rubber compounds that will allow better traction for cornering and acceleration - but the tires will tend to wear out faster.

Not only is the wheel offset insufficient on this car (wheel sticks out too far), but the tire is actually too narrow for the rim, making the rim stick out of the tire (tacky!)

As you can see, tire design is compromise. No one tire design can do everything well. Think about how much you really want to spend on your tires and wheels, including how often you can afford to replace the tires. If you choose the softer tread compounds for your tires, they'll have to be replaced perhaps twice as often as the original tires for your Focus. That adds up in the long run!

Think about ride quality, too. You may not be an old man with a bad back, but if you do a lot of driving, constant bumping and bouncing can be annoying. Remember that the ultra-low profile tires are not very practical if you do a lot of driving on rough roads. One good pothole hit is all it takes to damage the rim on a bucks-up wheel. A cheaper, higher-profile tire and wheel might absorb a hit from a pothole or curb just fine. The low-profile tires most often seen on sport compact cars that have been customized are going to ride rougher than the OEM rubber, since they have less "cushion" than higher aspect ratio tires. There's just no way around making a real compromise in tire selection.

If you do most of your driving on the street in normal traffic and on the highway, take a closer look at the sidewall markings while you're out tire shopping. First of all, the tire must have a DOT (Department of Transportation) number on it. If there's no DOT number, the tire isn't legal for the street and can only be used for racing on a track. Among the many numbers/letters/codes on the side of street-legal tires are the ratings of that tire for traction, wear and temperature. The ratings are in letter form, with A being the highest rating. It's difficult for a tire to make "straight A's" in every category, but to stretch your tire dollars, make sure you examine the treadwear rating. Likewise, for vehicles that see track action, temperature and traction ratings will be the categories you want your tire to score highest in.

So don't just go into a showroom and point to the wheels and tires that look the best - with that level of research, you're almost sure to be disappointed. Talk to the salespeople and technicians at the tire store and find out about the ride quality and treadlife of each tire, as well as its cost. Tire technicians who install a lot of tires can help you figure out how big a tire/wheel combination you can fit in your car. And if you're planning on lowering the car, tell them about that, too, since it will have an effect on maximum tire size. When in doubt about maximum tire size, contact the tire manufacturer for their recommendations.

Among the important markings on a tire are these ratings for Treadwear, Traction and Temperature performance

Race tires look cool, but don't get caught on the street without a legal-for-street DOT (Department of Transportation) indication or you could get a ticket

Some high-performance tires are "directional" in their design - the arrow marking means it must roll in this direction only, so you can't rotate these tires side-for-side

The most important markings on a tire are these for the tire size, profile and speed rating

Many people try to measure their own wheelwells with a tape-rule to determine how much clearance they have for larger tires and wheels. Even if you take these measurements with the front wheels in their extreme turn positions, there are many other variables that are very hard to calculate. For example, the new wheels will likely have more offset than your existing wheels. Overall tire-and-wheel height and width will be different than the wheel measurements themselves. And don't forget about suspension movement - you don't want to have the tires rub every time you go over a bump! No, it's best to let the experts determine your maximum tire and wheel size, and they are usually happy to help. And if the combination doesn't work, you'll have someone to blame besides yourself!

Enthusiasts who do their own research generally make better buying decisions, and on wheel/tires you need to look at all the examples of modified Focuses you can. Check out their tires and wheels and see not only how they look, but also how evenly they are wearing in the application. Look at the backside of the front tires, if possible, and see if the tire or wheels has been rubbing on any suspension or body parts. If the outside edge of the tire's tread is chewed or worn excessively, it could indicate this wheel/tire combo is too wide for the vehicle. Always compare "apples to apples." If the Focus you really like has a body kit or flares on the fenders, don't assume that the wide tires he's sporting are going to fit your stock Focus.

Tire size markings

All tires carry standard tire size markings on their sidewalls, such as **"195/60 R 15 87H"**.

195	indicates the width of the tire in mm.
60	indicates the ratio of the tire section height to width, expressed as a percentage. If no number is present at this point, the ratio is considered to be 82%. This section ratio is also called the aspect ratio or the "profile." A low number here means a low-profile tire that won't be as tall as a higher-ratio tire.
R	indicates the tire is of radial ply construction.
15	indicates the wheel diameter for the tire is 15 inches.
87	is an index number which indicates the maximum load that the tire can carry at maximum speed.
H	represents the maximum speed for the tire, which should be equal to or greater than the car's maximum speed.

Note that some tires have the speed rating symbol located between the tire width and the wheel diameter, attached to the "R" radial tire reference, for example, "195/60 HR 15".

Speed rating symbols for radial tires

Symbol	mph
P	93
Q	99
R	106
S	112
T	118
U	124
V (after size markings)	Up to 150
H (within size markings)	Up to 130
V (within size markings)	Over 130
Z (within size markings)	Over 150

Gallery of Wheels

06 Suspension

Altering you car's stock suspension can not only give you that lowered, aggressive look, but, if done right, will improve the handling as well.

Dropping the car on its suspension brings the car's center of gravity closer to its roll and pitch centers, which helps to hold it to the road in corners and under braking - combined with stiffer springs, shocks and stabilizer bars, this reduces body roll and increases the tire contact patch on the road. But - if improving the handling is really important to you, choose your new suspension carefully. If you go the cheap route, or want extreme lowering, then making the car handle better might not be what you achieve.

As for what to buy, there are basically four main options when it comes to lowering:

1 *Set of lowering springs.*

2 *Matched set of lowering springs and shock absorbers.*

3 *Set of "coilovers."*

4 *Air suspension.*

How low to go?

Assuming you want to slam your suspension so that your fenders just clear the tops of your monster new tires, there's another small problem - it takes some inspired guesswork to assess the required drop accurately and avoid the nasty rubbing sound and the smell of burning rubber. Lowering springs and suspension kits will only produce a fixed amount of drop - this can range from 3/4-inch to a more extreme drop of anything up to four inches. Take as many measurements as possible, and ask tuning shops or informed friends. Suppliers and manufacturers are also a good source of help. Coilovers have a range of adjustment possible, which can get you exactly the amount of drop you're looking for.

Suspension

High-rate lowering springs

For: This option is generally the least expensive way to go. You'll get the low-slung look and handling will be slightly improved.

Against: If your shocks are bad or your new springs are badly matched to their damping characteristics, handling could be poor.

Buy: Progressively wound springs which give a smooth ride but also cope with bumps, potholes and extreme cornering; springs for use with standard struts and shocks to prevent pogo-stick handling and shock damage; springs that offer a drop of between 3/4 and 1-1/2 inch - any lower will result in poor handling, fender-rub and excess tire wear.

Matched strut or shock/spring kits

For: Massive improvement in handling thanks to well-developed, matched springs and struts or shocks. Some have adjustable damping so you can fine-tune the ride quality. Price can range from fairly reasonable to through the roof!

Against: Due to increased damping and spring rates, the ride may be harsh.

Buy: Kits with progressive springs - these offer an improved ride without compromising handling; kits with adjustable shock damping; kits with multi-position spring platforms - enabling you to tweak the ride height.

Coilover kits

For: Ride height can be adjusted to the level you want. Most kits offer 3/4-inch to 4 inches of adjustment. Conversion kits are available for use with your stock struts and coil springs; these are generally only a little more expensive than a set of lowering springs. If you can afford to shell out the big bucks, you can go with a set of matched struts or shocks and springs with the threaded spring adjusters already installed on the strut bodies.

On some models, damping can be set as desired. The package can be set up to offer awesome handling on the road and then be dumped for shows and cruises.

Against: Coilovers can be hard to set up properly. If they're set to give a big drop, the springs can pop out of the top cups on full extension. Ride is hard - with a capital H.

Buy: Kits with helper springs - less spring dislocation; kits with adjustable damping.

Air suspension

For: Instant adjustability of ride height; great for dropping your ride when parked.

Against: Irregular ride and handling; possible damage to suspension components and body parts if not set up properly.

Buy: Complete kit with compressor, valves, struts (or damper units) and hoses.

Suspension

Suspension terms

Fender-rub
Fender-rub occurs when the suspension is too low or too soft. Going over a bump, the wheel is forced up as the suspension compresses, rubbing the wheel opening in the fender.

Circlip
The circlip is a flat, spring-steel clip that fits into a groove on the body of the strut or shock, on which the spring cup sits. On struts or shocks designed for lowering, there are sometimes a number of grooves offering differing ride heights.

Shock absorbers (shocks)/struts
A shock absorber absorbs the kinetic energy of the of the suspension during compression, or of the spring during rebound, damping further reaction from the spring. Shocks, as they're often called, stop the car from bouncing along the road, resulting in better handling. On cars with MacPherson strut-type suspension, the shock absorber and coil spring are incorporated into a strut that is also a structural member of the car's suspension that keeps the wheel in a vertical position. Many other cars have coil springs joined with the shock absorbers too, but upper and lower control arms handle the task of keeping the wheel upright.

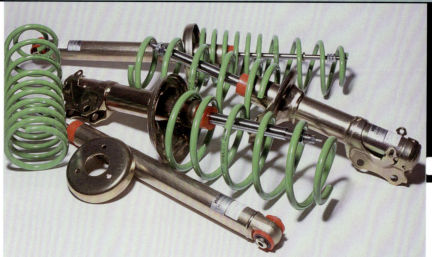

Damping
Damping is the action of the shock absorber dissipating energy when the suspension is compressed (such as when going over a bump) or during rebound (when the suspension extends after being compressed). On all modern motor vehicles damping is accomplished by forcing fluid through an orifice (or series of orifices).

Helper spring
Only found on coilover shocks or struts, the helper spring prevents dislocation of the main spring when it is unable to cope with extreme extension. The helper spring offers further extension travel, preventing possible dislocation.

Progressive wound
The coils on a progressive spring have been wound closer together at one end. This offers decent ride quality until the loose-wound coils are compressed, then, under further compression, the suspension is stiffer. This limits suspension travel and improves cornering without giving a harsh ride during normal driving.

Ride height
The ride height refers to the height of the chassis from the ground. The height of the springs determines the ride height and center of gravity.

Shot-peened
Shot-peening is a process in which tiny pieces of metal (shot) are fired at the surface of the steel spring, increasing the spring's surface area and making the spring stronger.

Spring cups
The spring cup is located on the body of the strut. The bottom of the spring sits in the cup with the help of an internal lug, which prevents dislocation.

Spring rate
The spring rate translates as the potential resistance against compression of the spring, measured in pounds. A low spring rate means the spring will give a better ride (is "softer"), while a high spring rate means the spring will "give" less and thus has a harsher ride.

Shock absorbers/ struts and coil springs

Replacing the struts and coil springs is an excellent way to lower a car. Although the car can sometimes be lowered by replacing the springs only, we recommend replacing the shock absorbers and strut assemblies with new ones specifically matched to the springs being installed. Doing this will help prevent fender-rub and result in better cornering. When done correctly, this conversion will get you lower but still retain predictable handling characteristics - this is a must if you like to push your car hard through corners.

Many aftermarket companies sell kits of matched shock absorbers/struts and springs, often referred to as a "suspension kit." Some of the kits are called "adjustable," but check this out carefully so you're sure you know what you're getting. With some kits this adjustment only applies to the damper rates of the shocks, which can be customized by simply turning a knob or screw on each shock or strut.

This feature has no effect on the ride height, but provides the ability to adjust for better ride quality or better handling. Other kits - the kind with threaded adjusters for the springs *and* damping adjusters for the shocks - offer the best of both worlds; ride height adjustment and damping adjustment. It's critical that you follow the instructions that will come with the parts. This is not a job for a beginner - if you don't know what you're doing, get help or have the job done for you.

Front strut/coil spring replacement

If you don't already have a *Haynes Repair Manual* for your specific car, now would be a good time to buy one. We'll take you through the basics here, but the *Haynes* manual will give you the details.

01 Loosen the wheel nuts, then raise the vehicle and support it securely on jackstands. First job is to unclip the brake hose from its bracket and pull the hose to one side, so it won't get damaged while you work. Tie it back if necessary.

02 Next, remove the stabilizer bar link nut and detach the link from the strut

03 Unscrew the strut-to-knuckle clamp bolt. This bolt is pretty tight, and you may have to squirt some penetrating oil to the other side (where the threads are) to help loosen it up. Also, penetrating oil applied around the strut body will help ease the next step

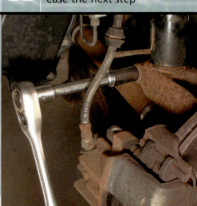

04 Now it's time to persuade that knuckle to detach itself from the strut. Use something to whack it with, but don't damage it!

05 You'll probably have to pry the control arm down to release the strut from the knuckle. We achieved this removal by using a big ol' prybar, some chain and a block of wood

06 Working in the engine compartment, remove the three strut upper mounting nuts. Don't touch the nut in the center of the strut - that's the piston rod nut (it keeps the coil spring and strut from flying apart!)

07 With everything loosened and removed, lift the strut from the vehicle - if it hasn't already fallen out! It's not a bad idea to place a jack under the control arm – that way you won't overextend the inner CV joint on the driveaxle

08 Use spring compressors and arrange these two clamps opposite each other. Tighten the clamps slowly and evenly; otherwise one of the springs may just try to escape - you definitely DON'T want that. Compress the spring until the tension is off the upper strut mounting plate

09 Next job is to remove the top mount plate and piston rod nut. Use an Allen wrench to stop the piston from turning or you will never get this nut off. You may need to re-use the top mount plate, so keep it handy for later

10 Remove the top mounting plate and upper spring seat . . .

Warning: *Disassembling a strut/coil spring assembly is potentially dangerous! Your full attention must be directed to the job, or serious injury may result. Before disassembling the strut, make sure you have a good spring compressor and obtain a new piston nut for each shock absorber (the nut should be replaced every time it is removed).*

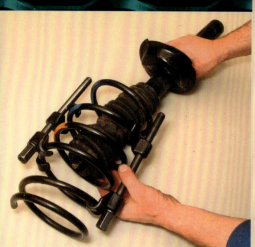

11 ... followed by the compressed coil spring. Keep in mind that the spring is still under major tension, so keep it away from your body (especially your head). When removing the spring compressor(s) from the coils, which is the next job, loosen them slowly and evenly or you'll end up having a very bad day!

12 Take the correct strut for the side of the vehicle you are working on and prep the piston by pulling it fully out. Then slip the washer (this particular strut uses something called a bumpstop protector – check to see if the kit you are using has one) onto the piston and install the bump stop. A new bump stop may be supplied with your kit, but it might be necessary to use the original one

13 Now its time to pop the shiny new spring into place. Use the correct spring (if it's not obvious which spring to use check the markings on the spring and refer to the manufacturers notes). Even if the springs look the same they may have different rates (stiffness), so check first

17 The newly assembled strut can now go back where it belongs. Hold it in place by loosely re-installing the three upper mounting nuts

18 Grease the strut brace to make future removal easier . . .

19 . . . then the pop strut back into the steering knuckle, making sure the raised section on the back of the strut aligns with the slot in the knuckle. Make sure the brake hose is kept out of the way to prevent it from being damaged. Jack up the assembly to meet the strut using the jack still in position under the control arm

14 The upper spring seat is the next part to be added to the strut. Due to the fact that our new springs are a lot smaller in width than the originals, we need to use an adapter spring seat (supplied with kit) into the original Focus top mount plate. Push this into place - it'll click when it has located properly

15 Pop the top mount assembly into place on the strut and fit the self-locking nut. Tighten it the same way it was loosened, by holding the piston rod with an Allen wrench

16 Set the ride height of the springs evenly on both sides (measure with a ruler); when you're finished with both sides you can do the fine-tuning, by lowering the car and checking out the clearance between the tires and the fenders and deciding if it needs to go up or down. You can then keep it level by simply turning the height adjustable and locking rings the same number of turns each side (which is a lot easier if you raise the vehicle one again and set it on jackstands)

20 Use a drop of thread locking compound on the clamp bolt . . .

21 . . . then tighten the bolt to the proper torque (refer to the Haynes Automotive Repair Manual for your Focus)

22 Clip the brake hose into its new bracket. If your kit does not have a bracket to attach the hose to the strut, you'll have to fabricate yourself a suitable bracket

23 Reconnect the stabilizer bar link to the bracket on the strut. Some cheap kits do not have holes for the link - if this is the case, you're on your own!

24 When tightening the stabilizer bar link nut, prevent the ballstud from turning by holding it with an Allen wrench

25 Reinstall the wheel and lower the car, then tighten the three upper mounting nuts to the proper torque (see your Haynes Automotive Repair Manual). After that, check out the car's attitude - the clearance between the fenders and the tires, how low it sits, etc., to see if it meets your approval. If not, read on

26 You can now set the ride height by winding the spring seat (height adjustment ring) up or down using the C spanners supplied. But understand, before doing this you really should raise the vehicle and support it on jackstands to take the weight of the car off the spring seats

27 When you've got your setting, counter-lock the adjustment ring in position with the lower (locking) ring

28 A bit of lube on the threads will aid future ride height adjustments

29 The final job is to adjust the damping as you see fit. Best to ensure that the shocks are not set too stiff, as the ride will be very harsh; remember with coilovers, the ride is quite harsh to begin with. Also, it's important that both sides are set to the same damping rate

Coilovers

If you've chosen matched shocks/struts/coil springs with "coilover" adjusters, you obviously know quality when you see it, and you're not prepared to compromise. True, quality costs, but you get what you pay for. This is an expensive option, but it offers one vital feature that others can't - true adjustability of ride height, along with proper damping rates and piston rod travel. This means you can get exactly the ride height you're looking for, but won't be bottoming-out your shock's piston rods like you would with a conversion kit.

Coilover conversion

Another option gaining popularity is the "coilover conversion." If you must have the lowest, baddest machine and want to save some money, these could be the answer. Offering as much potential for lowering as a genuine matched set of struts or shocks/coilovers, these items could be described as a cross between coilovers and lowering springs - the standard struts or shocks are retained (which usually results in less ride quality). What you get is a new spring and a threaded sleeve with an adjustable bottom mount - the whole thing slips over your standard strut or shock body. Two problems with this solution:

- Standard struts/shocks are not designed to operate as well when lowered, so the car's ride and handling will be compromised if you lower the car very much.
- The standard struts/shocks are effectively being compressed, the lower you go. There is a limit to how far they will compress before being completely solid. Needless to say, even a partially compressed strut or shock won't be able to do much actual damping - the result could be a very harsh ride.

Rear suspension

01 The first thing you are going to do is loosen the rear wheel lug nuts, raise the rear of the car and support it securely on jackstands. Go ahead and remove the wheels. Before beginning any disassembly of the suspension, it isn't a bad idea to spray some penetrating oil on all the fasteners you'll be dealing with

02 Unscrew the nut from the stabilizer bar link bolt and remove the bolt, bushings and washers (do this on each side). Keep the parts in order so you don't get confused when you go to put it back together

03 Recommendation: If you haven't upgraded your rear stabilizer bar yet, now is the perfect time. Unscrew the bushing clamp bolts and remove the bar. Keep in mind that it isn't necessary to remove the stabilizer bar to replace the coil springs, but why keep that anemic stock bar when you've dropped all your coin on new coils?

04 Just in case anything slips while you're lowering the spring (and it'll go with a bang if you're unlucky), make up a 'special tool'. Get yourself a sturdy metal strip, drill a hole in for a long bolt and nut, and fit it to the rear suspension as shown. The jack will do the lowering work, but this should stop it all from flying apart. Safety is what we're talking here

05 With a decent floor jack supporting the lower arm (compress the spring a little), unscrew the bolt at the outer end of the arm. Once that bolt is tapped out, the jack is the only thing stopping the spring from flying out, so take care

06 Loosen the nut on the special tool, then lower the jack slightly. Repeat this process until the spring pressure has been safely released

07 You'll find that the jack will want to move backwards as the spring is lowered, which might mean the lower arm jams up at the last minute. A little careful levering with the 'universal tool' (large screwdriver) should sort you out

08 Now the lower arm drops away, and the spring can come out. In case you were wondering why we didn't just use spring clamps to compress the old spring, and take it out that way - you can't. There's no room

09 The new springs are way easier to install than the old ones were to remove. So the lower arm can now go back up, and the outer bolt back in. Tighten this bolt to the proper torque (refer to your *Haynes Automotive Repair Manual*). Reinstall the stabilizer bar, too (if it was removed), and connect the links to the control arms

6-13

 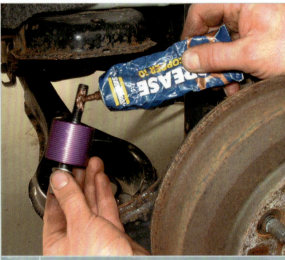 

10 The next job (at least on the kit we're installing) is removing this very large bolt from the top of the subframe (spring upper seat). We expected it to be rusted-in, but we were lucky - you might not be, so hit it with some penetrating oil first

11 This is why the bolt had to come out - to install the adjustable top mount for the spring. We lubed up the old bolt with a little grease before putting it back, and tightened it to the proper torque (we found that in our Haynes Automotive Repair Manual). This bolt holds the rear suspension to the car, so it's pretty important to get it tight

12 Screw the locking ring onto the threaded top mount, then add the new spring upper seat . . .

17 . . . then go into the luggage compartment and remove the upper mounting nut, holding the shock piston rod still with a smaller wrench if necessary . . .

18 . . . then take off the rubber mount - we'll be re-using that later

19 The shock absorber may have fallen off by this point, but if it hasn't, take it off. Slide off the other top mount, which we'll also be using

13 . . . while at the bottom end, the new spring lower seat gets hit with a bead of copper grease

14 Now for the transplant, which is so much shorter than the original spring, it's actually a very baggy fit. This is good, because it makes installation easy . . .

15 . . . but it's also bad, because the spring falls out just as easy. While the car was up in the air, we used a floor jack to lift the lower arm and hold the spring in place. It's obviously pretty important to check that the spring is located properly, top and bottom, when the car gets lowered back to the ground

16 Well, we've got a nice new spring, but what about the shock? Well, they're separate units on the Focus, so there's still some work to do. Unscrew the shock's lower mounting bolt . . .

20 This looks better already - a shiny new shock, complete with the top mount we just took off the old shock. Slide it into place, and tighten the bottom mounting bolt (to, yes, the torque listed in your Haynes Automotive Repair Manual). Back in the luggage compartment, reinstall the top rubber mount, then tighten the upper mounting nut

21 If you've installed adjustable suspension, get adjusting. When you've set one side (a best-guess job, first time), measure the height you set it to, so you can set the other side the same. Lock the spring seat in place with the locking ring - tighten them together with the two spanners provided. Treat the coilover threads to a little lube, to keep the rust at bay

22 You don't get a suspension kit with adjustable damping, and then not fiddle with it, do you? But - your new suspension's going to be way-stiff anyhow, so start out with a mild damping setting and see how it feels. Set both sides the same, to avoid getting strange handling quirks you can live without

Air suspension

Air suspension systems provide the ability to raise or lower the car instantly, from the driver's seat, or even from a distance on systems equipped with a remote control. Many consider this the ultimate suspension system, since you can lower the car as low as you want for shows and cruises, but still be able to easily raise the car to a reasonable ride height for your daily commute. The main components are air "springs" (which are basically strut assemblies with no coil springs) filled with compressed air. Pumping air into the air springs increases the air pressure and raises the vehicle, while releasing air from the springs lowers the vehicle. The system also has an electric air compressor, valves and air lines to deliver and release the compressed air. Air suspension systems also have a high-tech look: the compressors are often highly polished and sometimes chrome or gold plated - they can really dress up your engine compartment!

The primary disadvantage of an air suspension system, as you might have guessed, is cost: generally, they have a similar cost to coilover kits. And the ride quality and handling will never reach the level of a good, well-adjusted coilover kit - in fact, ride quality will likely be worse than with the stock suspension system. Another disadvantage is that the systems can cause damage to your vehicle's suspension and body if they are not set up and used carefully. The systems should be set up so that there will be no fender rub or metal-to-metal suspension bottoming when the air is released. Sometimes systems can leak down when the vehicle is left sitting for an extended period - you don't want to wind up with bent parts as a result.

There are a variety of air suspension systems available, and installation procedures vary. The air "springs" install basically the same way as standard struts or shocks. The air compressor is generally installed under the hood. Many owners choose to install a large separate storage tank for compressed air that allows rapid, repeated cycling of the system ("bouncing" the car up and down). When installing this equipment, refer to the manufacturer's instructions and recommendations.

Nasty side-effects

Camber angle and tracking

With any lowering "solution," your suspension and steering geometry will be affected - this will be more of a problem the lower you go. This will manifest itself as steering that either becomes lighter or (more usually) heavier, and as tires that wear out quickly on the inner or outer edges. If you've spent a small fortune on your wheels and tires, as most of us do, think carefully about this tire wear issue. Whenever you've installed a set of springs (and this applies to all types), have the wheel alignment checked ASAP afterwards.

The lower you set your suspension, the greater the inner edges of the tires will wear. This is because the camber setting becomes increasingly more negative the lower you go. Negative camber is when the top of the tires are closer together than the bottom. Some negative camber is good for hard cornering, but it's not something you want to live with on a daily basis. If you lower your car more than about 2-1/2 inches, you'll want to seriously think about installing a camber adjusting kit. No, they're not exactly cheap, but neither are those tires!

Strut brace

When you pitch your car into a corner hard, and then start sawing the wheel back and forth as you negotiate a tricky series of left and right hand corners, the loads imposed on the front end are considerable enough to actually twist the body, which will change the relationship of the strut upper mounts to each other. You don't want that!

If you've installed an aftermarket stabilizer bar, this problem could actually be *magnified*, because of the greater cornering forces you'll be imposing on the chassis. The camber and caster of the front wheels is established by the position of the upper ends of the struts. Allowing the upper mounting points of the struts to move means that the camber and caster are changing. A strut brace simply ties the two towers together and prevents them from flexing. And that's a good thing!

01 We're going to help out this Focus' handling by installing a strut brace. On the kit we're using, the first step is to remove the two inner strut upper mounting nuts from each side. Don't remove that nut in the center (between the strut mounting nuts) - that's the piston rod nut and it keeps the coil spring from flying out!

02 Place the strut bar mounts over the strut upper mounting studs, then install the nuts

03 Tighten the nuts to the proper torque specification (see the *Haynes Automotive Repair manual* for your vehicle)

04 As you have probably figured out already, you're done (and if this install took you longer than six minutes, you should be ashamed of yourself!)

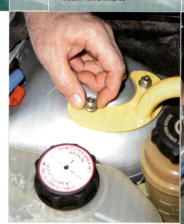

Installing a stabilizer bar

Even with stock suspension, most sport compact cars are fun to fling around. But their handling limitations become apparent when you start flicking them into corners a little harder than usual.

Stabilizer bars reduce the tendency of the car's body to "roll" (or tilt towards the outside of a turn) when cornering. Every Focus comes equipped with a stabilizer bar at the front, and some have one at the rear. But even if you have stabilizer bars front and rear from the factory, a good set of aftermarket performance bars will do you a world of good - you won't believe how flat your car will corner!

In the case of most front-wheel drive cars, installing a rear stabilizer bar (or replacing the stock bar with a thicker aftermarket one) is all you'll really have to do to get rid of (or at least greatly reduce) the inherent "understeer" characteristics that plague this type of drivetrain platform.

Replacing the front stabilizer bar bushings with aftermarket polyurethane ones will help that bar function more efficiently.

Installing a rear stabilizer bar

We'll show a typical install here, but make sure you follow the specific instructions that will come with the parts.

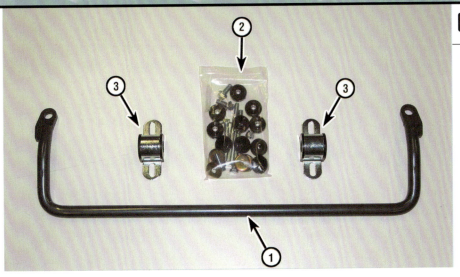

01 Unpack your stabilizer bar kit and make sure that everything you'll need is there. This kit includes a pair of polyurethane bar clamp bushings and a pair of links (to connect the stabilizer bar to the control arms). It also includes a small tube of special synthetic grease

1. Stabilizer bar
2. Links, mounting hardware and synthetic grease (for bushings)
3. Clamp and bushing

02 Raise the vehicle and place it securely on jackstands. Locate the stock link at each end of the stabilizer bar, then remove the nut, bolt, bushings and washers

03 Unbolt the bushing clamp from each side . . .

04 . . . then remove the stabilizer bar, bushings and clamps

05 Coat the insides of the new bushings with the special grease supplied with the kit.

08 . . . then install the bolts and tighten them securely

09 Now it's time to assemble the links and attach them to the control arms. On the kit we're installing, each link uses five bushings on each side. Begin by installing a dished washer onto the bolt, followed by a bushing (with the raised shoulder pointing up), then insert the bolt through the hole in the bar. Slide another bushing onto the bolt (with the raised shoulder pointing down), followed by another dished washer. Note: The concave side of each washer rests against the bushings

11 Next comes another bushing (it doesn't really matter which way the shoulder points), washer and bushing (the shoulder on this one must point up). At this stage, assemble the other link up to this point

11 Insert each link bolt through the hole in each control arm, then install the final bushing and washer (the raised shoulders on the bushings must point toward the control arms)

6-20

Understeer and oversteer

What exactly is "understeer"? And what is "oversteer"? A good understanding of oversteer and understeer is essential to anyone planning to upgrade the tires, wheels, coil springs and front and rear stabilizers.

Understeer

Understeer is the tendency of a car to slide off the road nose end first when you pitch it into a corner too hard. You turn the steering wheel as you enter the corner, but the car turns less than it should in response to the amount of steering input you're giving it. Most modern sport compact cars, particularly front-wheel-drive vehicles, are set up by the manufacturer for some understeer because at normal cornering speeds a bit of understeer feels safer and more predictable. But if you want your car to stick in the corners, you'll have to eliminate your car's understeer tendencies. One way to do that is to install a rear stabilizer bar or, if your car is already equipped with one, a bigger rear bar.

Oversteer

Oversteer is the tendency of a car to slide off the road tail-end first when you pitch it into a corner too hard. You turn the steering wheel as you enter the corner, but the car turns more than it should in response to the amount of steering input you're giving it. An oversteering car can be quick through the corners, but it can also be dangerous unless it's in the hands of a very skilled driver. Luckily, very few front-wheel-drive sport compact cars have an oversteer problem, because their weight distribution is invariably biased in favor of the front end.

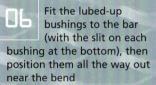

06 Fit the lubed-up bushings to the bar (with the slit on each bushing at the bottom), then position them all the way out near the bend

07 Raise the bar into position and fit the bushing clamps over the bushings . . .

12 Finally, install a nut on each link and tighten it according to the manufacturer's instructions. The sheet included with our kit said to tighten the nut until the top washer could no longer be turned by hand, then tighten it one more revolution

13 There it is. Nothin' fancy, and nobody's even gonna see it, but your Focus will be way more hooked up to the road!

07 Brakes

Brakes - the final frontier, or the biggest difference between a heroic high-speed charge and a humiliating high-speed crash. Here's what's what...

Brake pedal

Where it all starts, from your point of view. The pedal itself is a mechanical lever, and has to provide enough leverage to work the brakes if the power booster fails. Manufacturers use "brake pedal ratios" to express this - a low-ratio pedal, for instance, will give quick-acting but hard-to-work brakes.

Booster

The power brake booster on these vehicles is vacuum-operated, and it produces extra force on the pistons inside the master cylinder when the brakes are applied, reducing brake pedal effort. Most cars these days are equipped with boosters because they are also equipped with disc brakes (at least up front), and disc brakes require more force than drum brakes do (they aren't self-energizing).

Master cylinder

Below the brake fluid reservoir is the master cylinder, which is where the brake pedal effort (force) is converted to hydraulic effort (pressure), and transmitted to each brake through the hydraulic lines and hoses.

Brake fluid

Pressing the brake pedal moves the brake fluid through the lines to each brake, where the hydraulic pressure is converted back to mechanical force once more, as the pads and shoes move into contact with discs and drums. Fluid does not compress readily, but if air (which is compressible) gets in the system, there'll be less effort at the brakes and you'll get a fright. This is why 'bleeding' the brakes of air bubbles whenever the system has been opened is vital.

Brake hoses

For most of the way from the master cylinder to the wheels, the fluid goes through rigid metal brake pipes. At the suspension, where movement is needed, the pipes connect to flexible hoses. The standard rubber hoses are fine when they're new, but replacing old ones with great-looking braided hoses is a good move - in theory, it improves braking, as braided hoses expand less than rubber ones, and transmit more fluid pressure.

Calipers

These act like a clamp to force the brake pads against the discs - fluid pressure forces a piston outwards, which presses the brake pads onto the disc. Generally, the more pistons your calipers have, the more surface area the brake fluid has on which to push, providing greater clamping power. Most cars have only one or two per caliper, while exotic calipers may contain three, four or even more!

Discs

Clamped to your wheel hubs, the discs spin around as fast as your wheels. Over 90% of braking is done by the front brakes, which is why all modern cars have front discs - they work much better than drums, because they dissipate heat better. Many base models have "solid"

discs, while higher-performance cars have "vented" ones, which have an air gap between the braking surfaces to aid cooling. The bigger the disc diameter, the greater pad area available, with greater stopping power (think of a long lever as compared to a short one).

Pads and shoes

Both have a metal backing plate, with friction lining attached. Brake linings used to be made of an asbestos compound, which had excellent heat-resisting qualities but could cause cancer or asbestosis in people who breathed in the dust. Now they come in non-asbestos organic (stock), or for higher-performance applications, semi-metallic or carbon metallic.

Anti-lock Brakes (ABS)

Bottom line: Two cars are cruising down the road and a hay truck pulls out from a side road. Both drivers stand on the brake pedal. The car without ABS "locks up" the wheels and starts skidding, ending up sideways in a ditch. The car with ABS is able to slow down and safely maneuver around the truck. Great stuff, and here's how it works.

ABS works by detecting when a particular wheel is about to lock. It then reduces the hydraulic pressure applied to that wheel's brake, releasing it just before the wheel locks, and then re-applies it.

The system consists of a hydraulic unit, which contains various solenoid valves and an electric fluid return pump, four wheel speed sensors, and an electronic control unit (ECU). The solenoids in the hydraulic unit are controlled by the ECU, which receives signals from the four wheel sensors.

If the ECU senses that a wheel is about to lock, it operates the relevant solenoid valve in the hydraulic unit, which isolates that brake from the master cylinder. If the wheel sensor detects that the wheel is still about to lock, the ECU switches on the fluid return pump in the hydraulic unit and pumps the fluid back from the brake to the master cylinder, releasing the brake. Once the speed of the wheel returns to normal, the return pump stops and the solenoid valve opens, allowing fluid pressure back to the brake, and so the brake is re-applied. Pretty impressive, especially when you consider all this is happening in a fraction of a second! You may feel your ABS system working in a hard braking situation. The

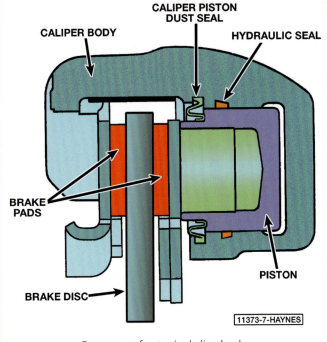

Cutaway of a typical disc brake

brake pedal will "pulse" as the pressure varies. But don't let up or "pump" the pedal yourself - let the ABS do its job. The rapid variations in fluid pressure cause pulses in the hydraulic circuit, and these can be felt through the brake pedal.

The system relies totally on electrical signals. If an inaccurate signal or a battery problem is detected, the ABS is automatically shut down, and a warning light on the instrument panel will come on. Normal braking will always be available whether or not the ABS is working.

ABS cannot work miracles, and the basic laws of physics will still apply: stopping distances will always be greater on slippery surfaces. The greatest benefit of ABS is being able to brake hard in an emergency without having to worry about correcting a skid.

If you have any problems with an anti-lock brake system, always consult an authorized dealer service department or other qualified repair shop.

Grooved and drilled discs

Besides the various brands of performance brake pads that go with them, the main brake upgrade is to install performance front brake discs and pads. Discs are available in two main types - grooved and cross-drilled (and combinations of both).

Grooved discs (which can be had with varying numbers of grooves) serve a dual purpose - the grooves provide a 'channel' to help the heat escape, and they also help to de-glaze the pad surface, cleaning up the pads every time they're used. Some of the discs are made from higher-friction metal than normal discs, too, and the fact that they seriously improve braking performance is well-documented.

Cross-drilled discs offer another route to heat dissipation, but one which can present some problems. Owners report that cross-drilled discs really eat brake pads, more so than the grooved types, but more serious is the fact that some of these discs can crack around the drilled holes after serious use. The trouble is that the heat 'migrates' to the drilled holes (as was intended), but the heat build-up can be extreme, and the constant heating/cooling cycle can stress the metal to the point where it will crack. Discs which have been damaged in this way are extremely dangerous to drive on, as they could break up completely at any time. Only install discs of this type from established manufacturers offering a useful guarantee of quality, and check the discs regularly.

Performance discs also have a reputation for warping (nasty vibrations felt through the pedal). Justified, or not? Well, the harder you use your brakes, the greater the heat you'll generate. Okay, so these wicked discs are meant to be able to cope with this heat, but you can't expect miracles. Cheap discs, or ones which have been abused over thousands of miles, will warp.

Performance pads can be mated to any brake discs, including the stock ones, but are of course designed to work best with heat-dissipating discs. Unless you plan on regularly participating in your club's track day, or hit the autocross circuit frequently, don't be tempted to go much further than 'fast road' pads - anything more competition-orientated may take too long to come up to temperature on the road. Remember what the brakes on your old ten-speed bike were like in the rain? Cold competition pads feel the same, and at regular street speeds may never get up to their proper operating temperature.

Lastly, installing all the performance brake parts in the world is no use if your calipers have seized up. If, when you remove your old pads, you find that one pad's worn more than the other, or that both pads have worn more on the left wheel than the right, your caliper pistons are sticking. Sometimes you can free them up by pushing them back into the caliper, but this is a sign that you really need new calipers. If you drive around with sticking calipers, you'll eat pads and discs. You choose.

Upgraded
discs and pads

Upgraded discs and pads are often the first step to a high-performance brake system, a simple modification that takes a couple of hours max, and can make a huge difference. Since they do wear down over time, and are also prone to warpage, there's a chance you'll have to change your discs anyway, so why not upgrade them at the same time?

Warning: *The dust created by the brake system is harmful to your health. Never blow it out with compressed air and don't inhale any of it. An approved filtering mask should be worn when working on the brakes. Do not, under any circumstances, use petroleum-based solvents to clean brake parts. Use brake system cleaner only!*

01 Unscrew the cap from the brake fluid reservoir and remove about two-thirds of the fluid, because when you perform the next step the fluid's going to rise, and if you don't take some out it'll overflow

02 Loosen the wheel lug nuts, raise the front of the vehicle and support it securely on jackstands. First job is to push the caliper piston back into its bore to make room for the new pads; you can do this with a large C-clamp. If you're working on a rear caliper with an integral parking brake actuator, you'll have to rotate the piston to get it to go down (you can engage the tips of a pair of needle-nose pliers with the slots in the piston face). Watch the brake fluid level in the master cylinder reservoir - don't let it overflow

03 Remove the plugs covering the caliper mounting bolts . . .

04 . . . then unscrew the caliper mounting bolts . . .

05 . . . and lift off the caliper. You won't be able to remove it completely, as it's still attached by the fluid hose - don't allow the caliper to hang by the hose!

Some good things to know about brakes

- Brakes create a lot of dust from the friction linings. Although usually not made from asbestos (very bad stuff) anymore, the dust is still something you'll want to avoid. Spray everything with brake cleaner and don't blow it into the air where you'll breathe it.
- Brake fluid is nasty stuff - poisonous, highly flammable and an effective paint stripper. Mop up spills promptly and wash any splashes off paintwork with lots of water.
- Do not use petroleum-based cleaners and solvents on or around brake parts. It will eat away all the rubber parts and hoses. Use only brake cleaner.
- Most brake jobs you can do without loosening or removing the fluid hoses and lines. If you mess with these you'll let air into the system and then have to "bleed" the brakes, which can be tricky. If you finish your job and then step on the pedal and it goes all the way to the floor, or feels soft or "spongy," you've let air into the lines.
- Which brings up a good point. After working on your brakes, start the car and pump the pedal a few times to bring the pads into contact with the discs, and to make sure all is well before charging down the street.

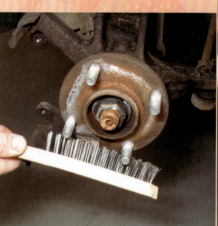

09 Any rust on the hub now has to go, along with any other crud. If the wheel hub isn't totally pristine, the new disc won't sit on quite straight, and will eat its way through the new pads in no time. So do it right and take a wire brush to the hub flange

10 If you want to spare yourself the misery of stuck-on discs in future, a little copper grease on the hub flange will be a big help

06 To remove the inner pad, simply pull it away from the caliper piston until the retaining clips disengage

07 To remove the outer pad, pry each end of the retaining spring from the caliper frame, then slide the pad out (not all models have this wire-type retaining spring; some only have the two spring steel arms that attach to the center of the pad backing plate). If you're just replacing the pads, skip to Step 12. But we hope you're more dedicated than that!

08 The old disc should slip right off the hub, but if it doesn't, a little persuasion with universal speed wrench (hammer) will usually do the trick

11 Like the hubs, the new discs must be clean before installing - give 'em a squirt of brake cleaner and wipe them down with a rag. Your new discs probably are not identical, and should only be installed with the grooves facing a certain way (this is the left front). Check the paperwork that came with your discs

12 Now for the new pads. Start by pushing the retaining clips of the new inner pad into the piston

 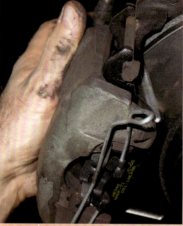 

13 Next, install the outer pad to the caliper frame, making sure the spring steel arms engage properly

14 Place the caliper and pads over the new disc and onto the steering knuckle. Make sure the ears on the ends of the pads rest on the bosses on the steering knuckle . . .

15 . . . then swing the retaining clip down and snap it into place over the caliper frame

> ⚠ **Caution:** New pads of any sort need careful bedding-in (over 100 miles of normal use) before they'll work properly - when first installed, the pad surface won't exactly match the contours of the disc (even if the disc is new) so it won't actually be touching it over its full area. This will most likely result in a set of very under-whelming brakes for the first few trips, so take it easy for awhile.

16 Clean, then lubricate the caliper mounting bolts with high-temperature brake grease, then install and tighten them to the proper torque (see your Haynes Automotive Repair Manual)

17 Much better! Now give the brake pedal several good pumps to bring the new pads up to the new disc, then check the brake fluid level in the master cylinder reservoir, adding some if necessary. Install the wheel and lug nuts and you're ready for a road test. When you've done both sides, that is. Your calipers may be slightly different than these - if so, refer to the Haynes manual for details

Painting calipers

Installing custom rims means that your brakes can be seen by anybody - not a problem usually, but if you've got massive wheels, you really need something good to look at behind them. So if you can't stretch to a big disc conversion or even upgraded pads and discs, why not clean up what you've got there already?

You can spray them or hand-paint them, but either way the key is in the prepping. Brakes are dirty things, so make sure they're really clean before you start.

We know you won't necessarily want to hear this, but the best way to paint the calipers is to do some disassembling first. The kits say you don't have to, but trust us - you'll get a much better result from a few minutes extra work.

⚠ Warning: *The dust created by the brake system is harmful to your health. Never blow it out with compressed air and don't inhale any of it. An approved filtering mask should be worn when working on the brakes. Do not, under any circumstances, use petroleum-based solvents to clean brake parts. Use brake system cleaner only!*

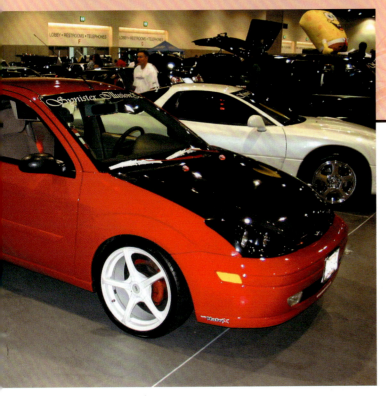

01 Remove the caliper, but leave the disc in place (if you don't know how to take the caliper off, see *Upgraded discs and pads*). Getting stuff clean is the name of the game, and you'll do a way better job with it all apart. Start off with a thorough soaking with brake system cleaner . . .

02 . . . then attack the caliper with a stiff wire brush. Get it as shiny as you can, then rinse it off with more brake cleaner (don't just spray it and leave it - get wiping as soon as possible. If you don't get it spotless, you'll get black streaks in the paint later, which will ruin all your hard work)

03 Mask off the brake hose, piston and its boot with tape - you don't need or want any paint on these parts. Also cover the brake disc and the surrounding areas with paper or a drop cloth to catch the overspray

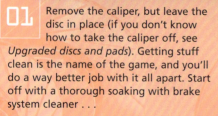

Tricks n' tips
If you have trouble reassembling your brakes after painting, you probably got carried away and put on too much paint. We found that, once it was fully dry, the excess paint could be trimmed off with a knife.

04 We found the best way to paint was to hang the caliper with an old coathanger (don't let the caliper hang by the hose!), and we used another piece of coathanger to serve as a handle. Now start sprayin' the color - several light coats will give you a better result than one heavy one, so be patient

05 Wait until the paint is totally dry (like overnight, or longer) before reassembling. Also make sure you tighten the caliper mounting bolts to the proper torque (see your *Haynes Automotive Repair Manual*)

01 At least there's no disassembling the drums - just raise the rear of the vehicle, support it securely on jackstands and remove the wheel. Now clean off the drums with brake system cleaner and a wire brush . . .

02 . . . then hit it with the brake cleaner one more time and wipe it down with a clean rag

03 You definitely don't want any paint on the wheel studs or where the wheels will touch the drum, so mask off the flat area on the drum . . .

Painting drums

04 . . . and the wheel studs, then place paper or drop cloth behind the brake to catch the overspray

05 Now start squirtin' the paint - once again, several light coats gives a better finish than one thick, sticky, runny coat. *Capice?* Thought so. Another good idea is to release the parking brake and turn the drum half a turn every so often until the paint is dry

06 Now we're talkin'!

Engine performance

The sign in the old performance shop used to read "Speed costs money . . . how fast do you want to go?" and it's just as true today. More important even than cost is organizing your modifications as a "package" of planned mods that work efficiently together.

Remember also that speed can cost you in other ways. An engine built to make 600 horsepower at the racetrack is not going to idle smoothly, get good gas mileage or go 200,000 miles between overhauls. Performance modifications are frequently called "upgrades," but we need to keep in mind that the performance end of the operational spectrum is what's being upgraded, and often you'll have to give up some of the smooth, reliable and economical operation that sport-compact cars are famous for.

So it's best to have a plan for your project, even if you don't have all the money to do everything right away. Don't plan on having a 9-second car that you can

Mistake number one

Ya gotta have a plan! The most common mistake when young enthusiasts start to modify their sport compact cars is getting dazzled by cars seen at shows or in magazines. This leaves the temptation to just start "throwing parts" at your car in an effort to be as cool or fast as those show cars. Every level of performance for your car should be a coordinated effort. Let's say there are several "phases" in your path to performance. In Phase One, you make several modifications that are all at the same "strength" of improvement. A "Phase Four" camshaft designed for very high rpm will do what it's designed for, but only when used along with a number of other modifications suited to that level.

Don't mix parts designed for different levels of performance! Have a performance goal in mind that is a realistic compromise for your driving needs and budget. If you really demand maximum horsepower, and you're willing to upgrade your drivetrain and lose a lot of driveability, then make your plan to use only Phase Four components. If a realistic plan for you is modifying your engine only to Phase Two, then only make those mods, nothing further.

Many enthusiasts start out buying parts that really don't help their engine at the performance level they're seeking. For instance, an aftermarket ignition system will add nothing to your relatively-stock engine except looks. The stock ignition works fine for most purposes, so unless you're building to a high level, you don't need the hot coil and amplifier. However, when you get to the higher stages, that performance ignition system will be required in order to fire the engine at high rpm with the increased cylinder pressure of a power adder like nitrous or a turbo. The other side of that coin is that a Phase Four camshaft on a Phase Two engine may give you less desirable performance.

Planning ahead means you won't have a garage full of expensive parts you bought and then later took off when you changed to higher or lower-Phase parts because things didn't perform the way you expected.

still loan to your mom on grocery day - neither one of you will be happy. Most of us will want to build a car that is a compromise: a car that is fast enough to race on the weekend, but is still practical to drive to work every day. Many upgrades, such as an exhaust header, cat-back system, and air-intake tube give "free" horsepower, with the only compromise being more noise (or as we like to call it, "engine music"). These upgrades are also relatively inexpensive and are "no-brainers" for any sport-compact build-up.

When you get into nitrous, turbos and superchargers, you'll be spending more money and also getting into more risk of engine damage. Camshafts and cylinder head work will reduce your car's low-speed driveability and frequently decrease your gas mileage. Often, when these modifications are designed to increase high-rpm horsepower, you'll actually lose some low-rpm power.

The stock engine compartment is not really something you'd want to show off

Engine compartment dress-up

Open the hood on a sport compact car and what do you see? Black plastic air filter housing, black air intake duct, black battery, black radiator and heater hoses, black vacuum hoses, black fuse box, black electrical harnesses, black accelerator and cruise control cables, black valve cover (with, of course, a black oil filler cap), black . . . well, black everything. Black, black, black everywhere! A sea of black! It's as if the engine compartment was dressed for a funeral or some other somber occasion.

We took this Focus engine compartment from stock-and-filthy to attention-getting with inexpensive, easy-to-install parts from our local auto parts store. This Chapter shows you how we did it.

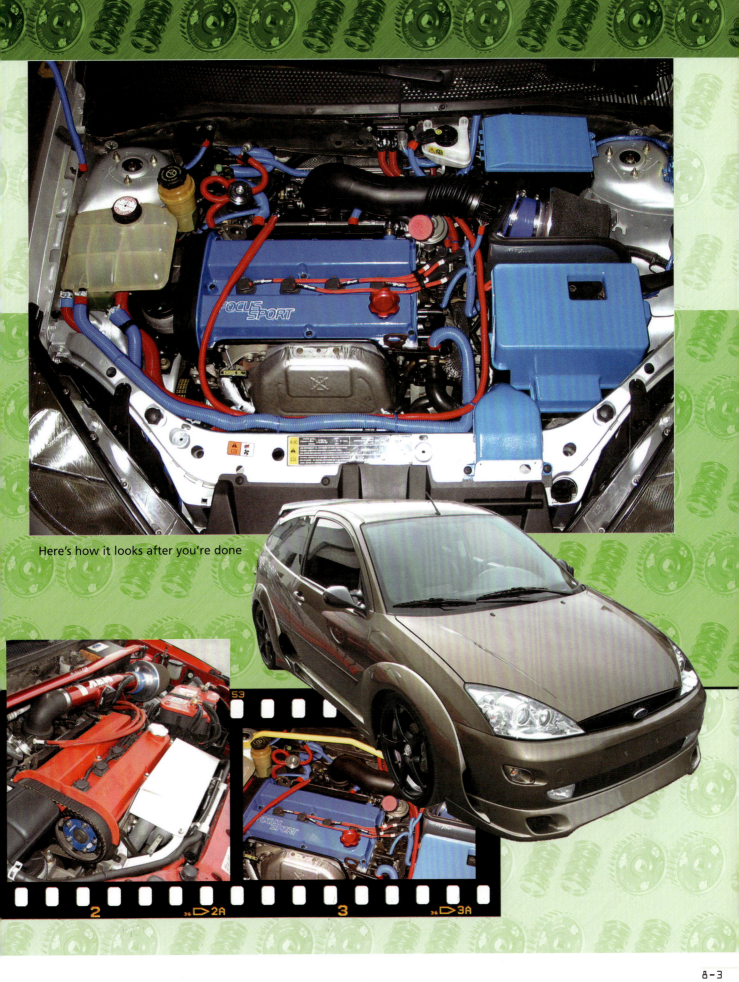

Here's how it looks after you're done

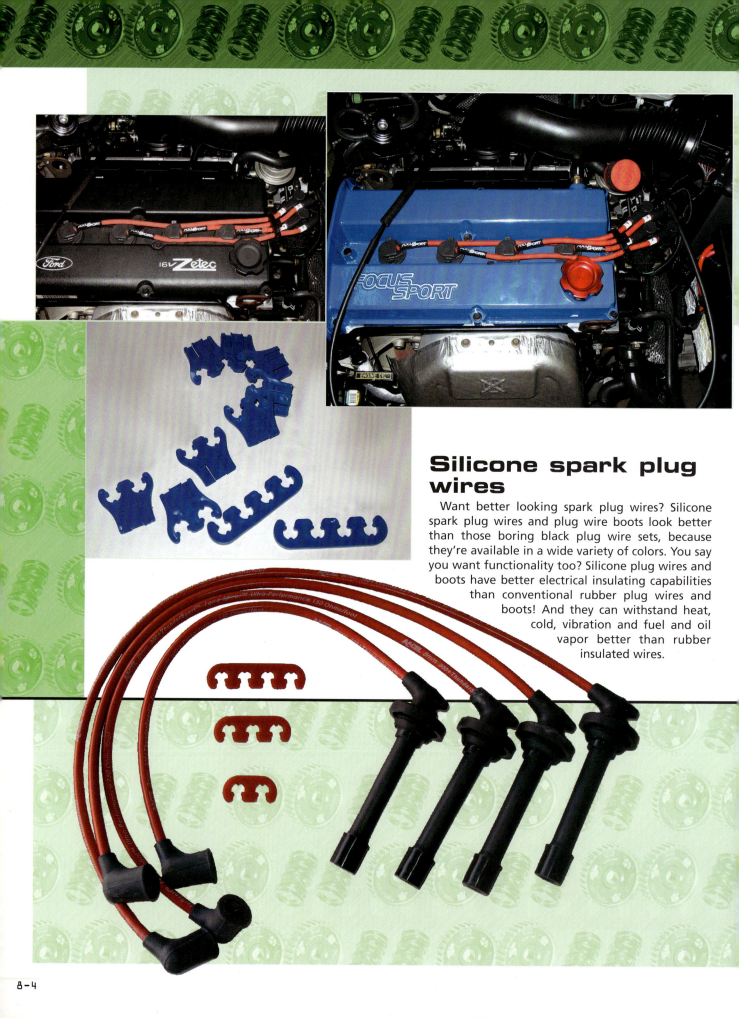

Silicone spark plug wires

Want better looking spark plug wires? Silicone spark plug wires and plug wire boots look better than those boring black plug wire sets, because they're available in a wide variety of colors. You say you want functionality too? Silicone plug wires and boots have better electrical insulating capabilities than conventional rubber plug wires and boots! And they can withstand heat, cold, vibration and fuel and oil vapor better than rubber insulated wires.

01 Disconnect the longest spark plug wire and boot from the number one spark plug and from its corresponding terminal on the coil pack. The boots on some vehicles are rather long, and sometimes difficult to disconnect. Do not pull on the wire itself; pull only on the boot

IMPORTANT NOTE!
Replace one spark plug wire at a time. If you mess up the order of where each wire goes, you'll be sorry!

02 Plug the new silicone spark plug wire into the same coil pack terminal from which you just disconnected the old spark plug wire . . .

03 . . . until you've replaced all four wires. Always finish one wire before disconnecting the next one. (You'll be able to tell which wire is for which cylinder, because they're four different lengths)

Silicone vacuum hoses

Remember when you could have any color vacuum hose you wanted . . . as long as it was black? That's not a problem with silicone vacuum hoses. They come in a dozen colors, so you can go with an all-red or all-yellow theme, or you can use an assortment of colors to denote various functions (red spark plug wires, yellow vacuum lines, blue coolant hoses, etc.). The possibilities are endless! Silicone vacuum hoses are available in all three common diameters (4 mm, 6 mm and 8 mm). You can buy starter kits that include an assortment of diameters, or you can buy lines individually, by the foot.

01 After finding a candidate for your hose swap, disconnect the stock hose. If it's really stuck, you may have to carefully slice it with a knife.

02 Cut the new hose to length and you're set. Just make sure the hose is a nice snug fit (the correct inside-diameter). If it's loose, you'll have a leak and your engine might not run right.

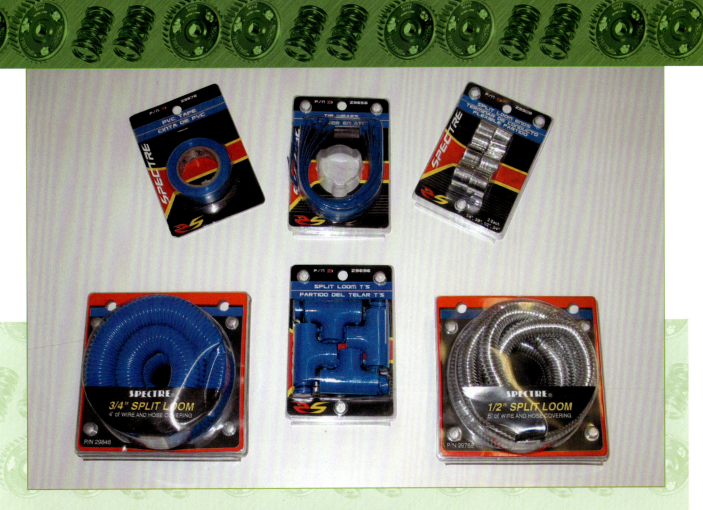

Split loom wire harnesses

Plastic split-loom is easy to install and looks great. It will help protect your wiring and is easy to remove for servicing. You'll never realize how many wires you have until you have to cover them - but don't worry, this one's easy!

01 If the harness or cable is already covered by the old black plastic stuff, remove it first

02 Install the new split loom and tape the end (the end that you're not going to cut) with matching electrical tape

03 Where wires go off in different directions, make a clean Y and tape

Braided metal hose covers

Braided covers are available from automotive retailers in a variety of lengths and diameters. Typical cover kits include six feet of material for vacuum lines, fuel hoses or heater hoses. Radiator hose covers are available in three or six foot lengths, each of which is available in 1-1/2 inch or 1-3/4 inch diameters.

Most aftermarket manufacturers of stainless-look braided cover kits also include anodized aluminum "clamps" which look just like the more expensive fittings used on race car plumbing. Except that they're just aluminum rings, machined to look like big nuts, which fit over a standard hose clamp (which you can easily hide by putting it on the side of the hose that nobody will ever see).

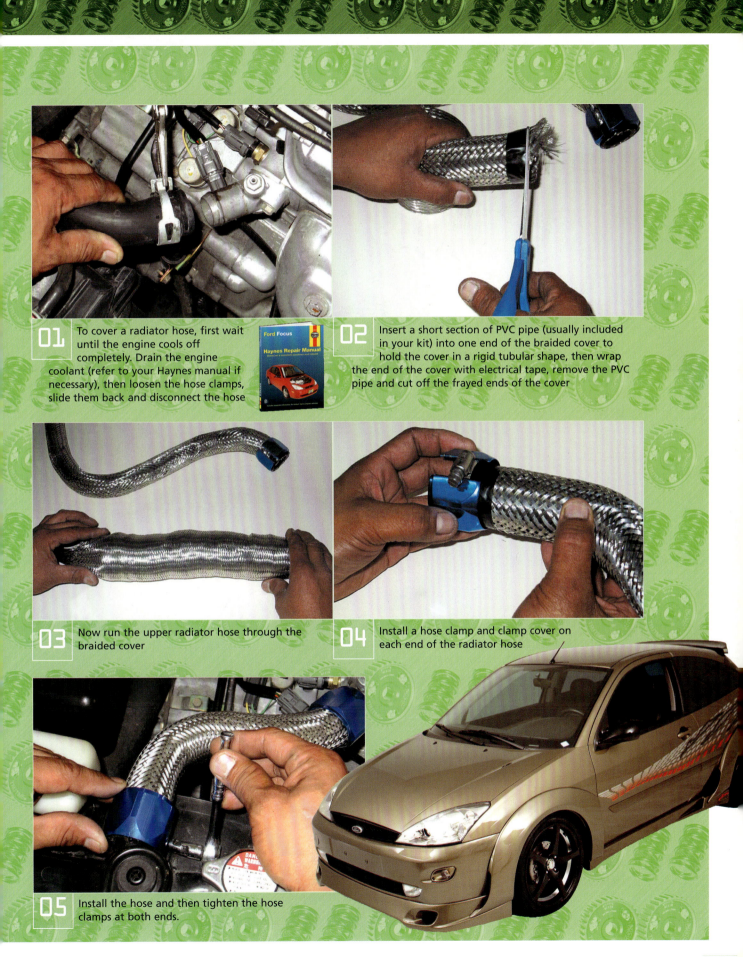

A little fresh paint

No matter how pretty your engine compartment might look by now, all those black covers and brackets are always going to be an eyesore. Why not simply paint some of the more prominent pieces to match your engine compartment color scheme?

Painting covers

 We decided to brighten things up by painting the black underhood covers. First remove them, clean them well and spray them with primer

 After the primer is fully dry, smooth and prepare the surface with 1000-grit sandpaper, using plenty of water

 When the primer is fully dry, spray on the color coat. Two coats may be necessary

01 After removing the spark plug wires and breather hose, unscrew the upper valve cover bolts

02 At the front of the timing belt cover, remove the four bolts, then pull the cover away from the cylinder head enough to allow valve cover removal

Custom valve cover

On some cars, the valve cover may be hidden by other engine components or a plastic engine cover of some kind, but on the Focus the valve cover is gloriously on display at the center of the engine compartment – why not make it beautiful!

Since you've probably got a plastic valve cover on your Focus, it make sense to replace it with an aftermarket one that's aluminum. We chose a nice one from FocusSport that's blue, which looks really good with our red-anodized oil filler cap and red plug wires.

03 Lift up the valve cover – if its stuck, do not try to pry under it with a sharp object, as this will damage the aluminum in the cover and cylinder head – bump the cover loose with a rubber mallet if necessary

04 Make sure to install a new sealing gasket in the custom valve cover – guide it carefully and slowly into the groove all around – this is a good design for ideal engine sealing

05 Install and tighten the cover bolts by hand at first, then go around and torque them to 60 in-lbs (which isn't much!), working from the center of the pattern outward, then secure the top of the timing belt cover

Modifying exhaust

Of all the "bolt-on" modifications you can make, improving the exhaust system is one that pays benefits in several areas, regardless of the "Phase" of performance you're after. Once you have a free-flowing system, it'll work with all future mods.

When you assemble the right package of exhaust components that allow your engine to really breathe, the car's going to sound as good as it performs. It bears repeating here that the exhaust system is one of the few aspects of modifying that gives you the performance you want without any of the drawbacks or compromises that usually come with engine mods. On the contrary, the exhaust work should have no effect on your idling or smooth driveability, and your fuel economy will actually go up, not down! The cool sound is a bonus, too.

Header design is an inexact science, most of what we know is through trial and error, but basically the idea is to have the right size and length pipes and arrange them so each pipe complements the others in terms of timing - this example is a popular sport-compact 4-2-1 design where four pipes become two, then two pipes become one to connect to the system

As you can see here, on a non-SVT Focus, the location of the catalytic converter precludes the legal use of a long header because you can't relocate the converter to under the car

The classic performance muffler is a straight-through design, in which there is a perforated core surrounded by fiberglass sound-dampening material (Airmass Thundermuff shown) – they used to be called simply "glasspacks" and have always been noted for their performance sound

If you're racing a Focus and street-legality isn't an issue, you can take advantage of this four-into-one, long-tube race header from FocusSport

Backpressure and flow

Even a stock engine that operates mostly at lower speeds has to get rid of the byproducts of combustion. If it takes fuel and air in, it has to expel those gasses after the reciprocating components have turned the cylinder pressures into work. The exhaust system needs to allow swift exit of those gasses, and any delay or obstruction to that flow can cause engine efficiency to suffer. If there is an exhaust flow problem somewhere in the system, the pressure waves coming out with the gasses can "back up," which can cause the cylinders to work harder to complete their four-stroke cycle. In exhaust terms, this is called backpressure, and getting rid of it is the chief aim of performance exhaust system designers.

We know that the right-sized length of straight pipe, with no catalytic converter and no muffler, would probably offer the least backpressure to the engine, but it's not very practical (or legal) for a street-driven machine. For our purposes, we have two main components between the exhaust valves and the tip of the tailpipe: the header, and everything from the catalytic converter back (which includes the converter, exhaust pipe, silencer, tailpipe and muffler). If we can improve flow both ahead of and behind the converter (which we must keep to be legal), we'll have the best street exhaust system possible.

Headers

The first major component of your performance exhaust system is the header, a tubular replacement for your stock cast-iron exhaust manifold. In most OEM sport compact applications the stock exhaust manifold isn't too bad, at least for the needs of your stock economy engine. The exhaust flow needs of an engine go up exponentially with the state of performance "tune." The flow and backpressure needs of a stock engine aren't excessive, especially when the engine spends the bulk of its driving life under 4000 rpm. But what happens when you modify the engine and then take advantage of those modifications by using the high end of the rpm scale? The exhaust system that was once adequate is now restrictive to a great degree.

How much power you make with just the header depends on several factors. On a car with a really restrictive stock exhaust system, particularly an exhaust manifold full of tight bends and twists, the header will make a bigger improvement than on a car with a decent system to start with. What's behind the header can make a big difference as well. If the stock exhaust system includes restrictive converter and muffler designs, small-diameter exhaust pipes and lots of "wrinkle bends" to boot, the header isn't going to have much chance of making a big improvement in performance. A good header on a typical Focus engine with few other modifications can be expected to make only 3-5 horsepower, depending on how good or bad the stock manifold had been. That's with a stock exhaust system from the header back.

If you have lowered your car quite a bit, you might consider using a system with an oval-shaped muffler rather than round – the oval muffler and oval tip doesn't hang down as low as a large round muffler, giving you clearance to still get up steep driveways or over speed bumps without scraping

That sounds disappointing, but if we take a case where the engine has numerous modifications yet still has a stock exhaust manifold, the same aftermarket header could gain 10 horsepower. Any of the big "power-adder" modifications, including nitrous oxide and supercharging virtually "require" a header and free-flowing exhaust system to take advantage of their power potential.

Installation of a performance header is quite easy. Most aftermarket headers are made to use all the factory mounting points and braces. In fact, beware of one that doesn't because the header may sound "tinny" when installed if the proper braces aren't connected. Make sure before buying a header that you give the shop your exact year and model. Most headers we've seen do not have provisions for bolting on the factory tin heat shield over the header, but we're pretty sure you want to show off your new pipes anyway.

If you have a regular Focus, the stock exhaust design is not aimed at performance. The location of the catalytic converter is right up next to the exhaust manifold, rather than down under the car. Since you can't relocate the converter (at least you can't do that and pass the emissions tests in most states) then a header designed for the Focus has to duplicate the stock manifold, with very coiled-up pipes that go up and then turn right back down to meet the converter. An aftermarket header for your Focus may make less of an improvement than a long header would for those "other" sport compact cars. The SVT Focus was designed for performance, so the cat was placed under the car to accommodate a nice long header for reduced backpressure.

01 The stock exhaust system is welded together on the assembly line, so the only way to remove it is to make a cut just ahead of the rear wheels – an old trick in tight confines is to turn the blade around in the hacksaw handle and, in this case, cut downward

Cat-back system installation

Once the exhaust gasses leave your exhaust manifold, they must travel a ways to get out from under your car, and our goal is to make it more of a freeway than a mountain road. First off, there is the catalytic converter, usually bolted right there to your manifold. For most of us, this is not an optional component because we have to have it to pass emissions tests. That's fine, because the converter does do a great job of cleaning up engine emissions, and the designs of current converters are more free-flowing than older ones, so the converter isn't something to whine about too much.

Most of the aftermarket exhaust systems are called "cat-back", because they include everything from the converter back. The system may be in several pieces to simplify packaging, shipping and installation, but it should bolt right up to the back flange of your converter and include whatever silencer(s) and muffler(s) are needed. Many of the cat-back systems include the muffler, which on most sport compacts is a part of the car that's very visible, especially when it's a really big one mounted right at the rear bumper.

The muffler you choose has a proportionately large share of both the sound level and backpressure of your total exhaust system. We all like a "good" growl or purr, but a really free-flowing muffler may be loud to the point of annoying. Maybe what we want is like the sound of a Ferrari: purrs at idle; draws attention when accelerating; and at full song it's like music. Some muffler companies actually have their mufflers divided into "classes," with one group having the "most aggressive" sound, another a little more subdued, and one that's described as

02 Lubricate all the rubber exhaust hanger "donuts", then use a prybar to get them off the body mounts – here we are prying off the one in front of the rear resonator (muffler) – don't lose the rubber tip, you'll need it later

03 At the rear of the resonator near the tailpipe tip, remove the rearmost rubber donut of the system . . .

"mellow." The perfect sound is such a subjective thing, you may want to just listen around when you're at events with a lot of sport compacts. When you hear a car whose tone suits you, check for a name on the muffler or ask the owner.

Changing the exhaust of your vehicle for a performance system is one of the modifications with more perks than almost any other. You get increased power, improved fuel economy, the sound that will complement your performance profile, and parts that make your ride look better, too. All that, and there's no real downside or sacrifice as with most engine mods.

04 . . . and lower the whole rear exhaust section rearward and out of the car

05 Spray WD-40 on all the donuts and all fasteners such as here at the front joint, then remove the two nuts at the flange

06 With a little oil, those rubber donuts at the front pipe will come off easily, especially since there is room to work here

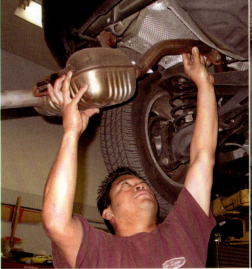
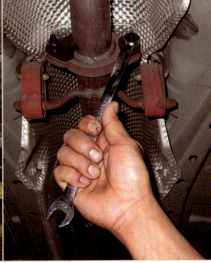
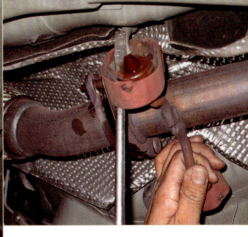

07 Now the bulk of the exhaust system can be removed from under the car – obviously, all of this work is a lot easier if you have access to a hoist

08 With the old parts on the shop floor, we can compare the layout of the stock exhaust with the new 2-1/4-inch diameter system from FocusSport, which has a skinny muffler up front, a large resonator ahead of the rear wheels, and a free-flowing pipe from there out – the whole system is coated with a shiny ceramic, high-temperature coating that may outlast your car

12 Secure the very rearmost section with the rubber donut . . .

13 . . . then place the stock copper gasket in position between the two flanges at the rear of the resonator and insert the bolts - put the washers and nuts on but tighten only finger-tight so far

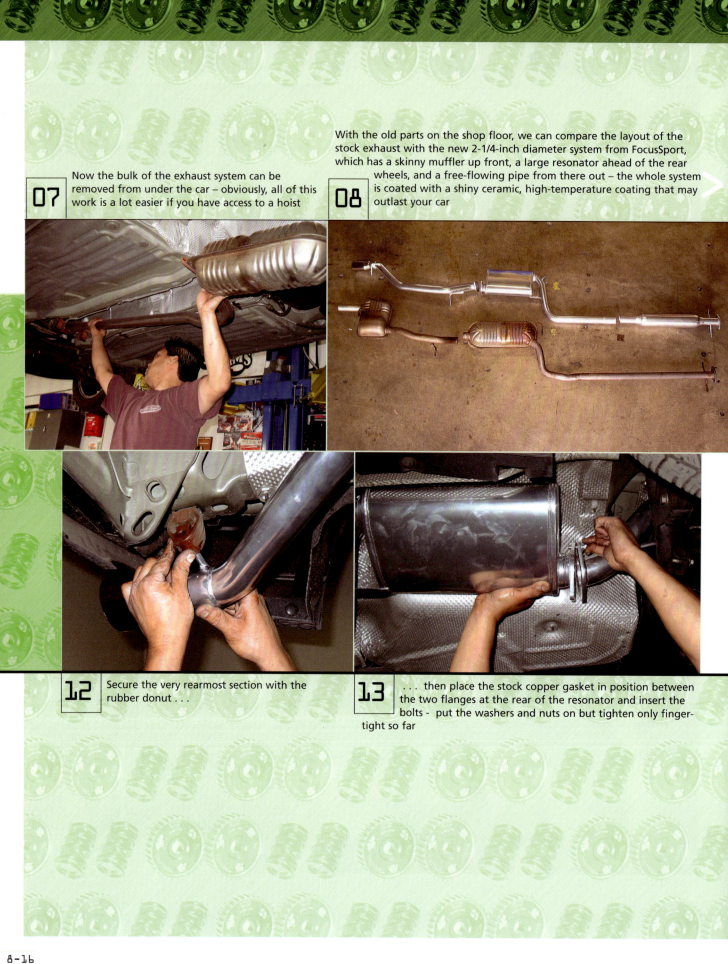

09 The front section of the system can be attached to the front donuts (make sure the pipe hangs as shown, not with the pipe below the prong-bar) with the gasket and the bolts loosely fastened for now

10 Lift up the middle section of the FocusSport cat-back and secure the rubber donut just ahead of the big resonator to hold this section in place – big pliers like these are very helpful in wrestling donuts over the prongs on exhaust hangers

11 Give the resonator a little "hang time" and insert the rear section of pipe up and over the rear suspension

14 We're really getting close now – there should be enough wiggle room to slip the front of the middle section (it's flared out) over the back of the front section and push the two pipes toward each other as far as they will go

15 Assemble the exhaust clamp over the junction of the two sections and, making sure the pipes stay aligned, tighten the nuts finger-tight

16 Now go back to the front of the system and tighten the front exhaust fasteners to specifications

17 We said you would need this rubber tip back at the resonator – it keeps the prong here from rattling against the chassis bracket if the system is jostled around on bumpy roads

18 Tighten the rear flange bolts at the resonator, then move up to the middle of the system and tighten the clamp

19 Here's the complete FocusSport performance cat-back installed and ready to make music – nothing hangs down, everything fits nicely without surprises and we get sound, mileage and performance

20 The end of the FocusSport system is a polished-stainless tip welded to the system – it's bigger than the stock tip but not "coffee-can" outrageous and fits the bumper cutout exactly. Here's a tip: Clean all fingerprints off the stainless steel tailpipe with rubbing alcohol or the smudges could become permanent

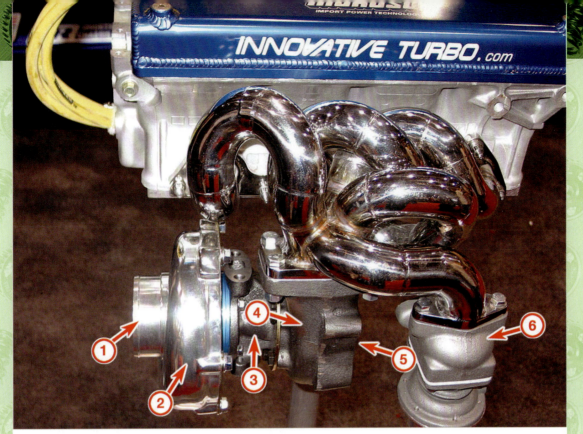

Seen here outside of the car is a Focus turbo setup that illustrates how all these components fit into the larger picture of a turbo setup: 1, the air intake of the compressor side; 2, the compressor housing; 3, the oil-cooled center housing; 4, the exhaust-driven turbine side; 5, the turbine outlet (where exhaust connects to the system downpipe); and 6, the wastegate that controls the maximum boost level

Turbochargers

Of the three major "power adders" (nitrous oxide, superchargers, and turbochargers), the turbocharger offers the biggest power potential of all. Its durability and practicality has been proven many times over on production cars and trucks worldwide, whenever extra power was needed without the trouble and expense of fitting the vehicle with a bigger engine.

How it works

There are basically three main elements to a turbocharger: the exhaust turbine, the intake air compressor, and the housing/shaft/bearing assembly that ties the two pressure-related sections together. The job of the turbine is to spin the shaft of the turbocharger. The turbine is composed of an iron housing in which rotates a wheel covered with curved fans or blades. These blades fit precisely within the turbine housing. When the turbine housing is mounted to an engine's exhaust manifold, the escaping hot exhaust gasses must flow through the housing and over the vanes, causing the shaft to spin rapidly. After the exhaust has passed through the turbine it exits through a large pipe, called a downpipe, to the rest of the vehicle's exhaust system.

Within the compressor housing is another wheel with vanes. Since both wheels are connected to a common shaft, the intake wheel spins at the same speed as the turbine, so the compressor draws intake air in and the rapidly spinning wheels blows the air into the engine's intake side. The more load there is on the engine, the more the turbocharger works to give the engine horsepower. As the engine goes faster, it makes more exhaust, which drives the turbocharger faster, which makes the engine produce more power.

The unit in the center of this turbo "sandwich" has the important function of reliably passing the power between the two housings.

Advantages and disadvantages of the turbocharger

Compared to the supercharger, the turbo is smaller, lighter, quieter, and puts less direct load on the engine. The "not at all times" boost of the turbocharger is an advantage for fuel economy, operating noise level and driveability, but in some cases may be a drawback when compared to the mechanical supercharger. While a supercharger adds boost in relation to rpm (i.e. the faster the engine goes, the faster the blower pumps) it runs up against physical limitations eventually and can't pump any more. In order to make any more boost with a supercharger, you have to change the pulleys or gearing that drives it.

The limitation for the blower-equipped car is in top end performance, and this is where the turbocharger has the distinct advantage. The turbocharger is much more customizable, with various wheels and housings available to suit whatever the intended engine or purpose. Boost can be made to come in early, or come in later at a higher boost level.

The same basic turbocharger can be used for street use or modified to make more boost than your engine can live with! Such customizing, called sizing, should be done by an experienced turbo shop that can select the exact right components for your engine size and power requirements.

This typical complete turbocharger kit (Gude package for Focus) has all the good stuff, plus a set of performance fuel injectors, a computer upgrade, chromed piping, and an intercooler to mount down under the grille to cool the intake air before it enters the intake manifold

Turbocharging kits

A complete turbocharging kit from most reputable aftermarket companies will include virtually everything you need for your application, with a cost from $2500 to $4500 for the package. If the price of a good turbo kit sounds expensive, just compare turbocharging to other methods of upping your horsepower. A turbo could be your best horsepower-per-dollar investment. Installation will vary widely between different model cars and turbo kits.

Intercoolers

One of the serious disadvantages of the turbocharger is the heat it will put into the intake air charge, which is why most successful turbo systems utilize an intercooler to combat this. Air coming from the turbocharger tends to be hot because it's compressed and also because of its close proximity to the exhaust.

The most effective and common method of dealing with intake air temperature on a turbocharged car is an intercooler. This is a honeycomb affair much like a radiator, usually mounted out in front of the vehicle's radiator in an opening below the bumper where cooler air is found. The boosted air from the compressor is ducted through pipes and into the intercooler, and then to the intake of the engine. Thus, the cooler is between the compressor and the engine, so it's called an inter-cooler. Since cooler air is more dense and produces more power, intercoolers are very popular.

The main boost control device on a turbocharger is an exhaust wastegate – this is a selection of GReddy wastegates. The more the turbo system is designed to flow, the bigger the wastegate must be to be effective – the wastegate keeps the turbo from overspeeding (and the engine from blowing) by releasing some exhaust before it reaches the turbine portion of the turbocharger

A blow-off valve is like a wastegate for the intake side of the system – it prevents pressure surges in the intake tract when the throttle is suddenly closed (like when shifting) – most enthusiasts have their blow-off vented to the atmosphere so it makes a head-turning noise when it operates during shifting

Durability with a turbo

Problems with turbo installations usually crop up because of detonation caused by too much boost, or not enough fuel under boosted conditions. A turbocharged performance car can be both reliable and pleasurable to drive, even on a daily basis, if you keep in mind the limitations.

The low-octane of today's pump gas will be the biggest limiting factor on street-driven (non-race gas) machines. With a reasonable boost level of 5-10 PSI and the proper precautions, you can run pump gas. With an electronic timing controller, you can switch from one timing program to another depending on the octane rating of the gas you have available.

Proper fuel mixture is very important. One lean-out and you'll fry at least one piston or valve! Keep checking your spark plugs and have a good programmable piggyback fuel controller. A fuel pressure regulator that can handle boosted conditions, a boost-capable MAP sensor, and a fuel system that can deliver extra pressure under boost should keep things under control.

We can't address every aspect of turbocharging here, but other steps to improving durability include keeping the engine cool with the use of a good radiator and fan, external engine oil cooler, and of course an intercooler. If you consistently run high boosts, internal engine upgrades will have to be made, such as forged, low-compression pistons, forged aftermarket rods, improved-flow oil pump, and a blueprinted rotating assembly. You'll find yourself addicted to the whoosh under acceleration and the snarl when you shift and your blow-off valve dumps the excess pressure so that everybody knows you're under boost!

There's nothing like a supercharger to make a car come alive - research all your options and plan other mods to work with your new supercharger – this Focus has a Vortech blower with that company's air-to-water intercooler for a potent, yet compact installation

Superchargers

Your engine is in a constant state of combustion when running. It sucks in air and fuel, burns it to make the pistons go, then expels what's left. With a supercharger, instead of having to use its own energy to suck in the mixture, your engine is *force-fed*, and the difference can be worth 50% and more in horsepower. Boost is good!

A turbocharger is similar in function to the supercharger, but differs in that the turbo is driven by exhaust gasses, rather than by mechanical means. A supercharger (also called a blower) is driven by the engine, either with gears, chains or belts, so there is direct correlation between the engine speed and the boost produced by the supercharger.

While the turbocharger may have the upper hand when you're talking about all-out high-rpm performance on the track, the supercharger shines at improving street performance almost from idle speed on up. Low-rpm power is very helpful for "across-the-intersection" performance, where a turbocharger is probably just "spinning up" and not yet able to provide much power.

Some supercharger kits include a whole new intake manifold, like this Jackson Racing package going into a Ford Focus – This new intake will work better than adapting the blower to the stock intake

Boost

Boost is any pressure beyond normal atmospheric pressure (14.7 psi). So, if you have a turbo or supercharger that is making 14.7 psi of boost, then you have effectively doubled normal atmospheric pressure or added another "atmosphere." Twice that amount of boost and you've added two atmospheres, and you command the bridge of a rocket ship!

However, we must be realistic about boost levels. There is a finite limit to the boost your blower can make, and probably a much lower limit of how much boost your engine can take, regardless of how the boost was generated. You'll find most street supercharger kits are limited to 5-7 psi, to make some power while working well on a basically stock engine that sips pump gasoline.

Some kits on the market have optional pulleys that will spin the blower faster for more boost, but, as with any power adder, you can only go so far in increasing cylinder pressure before you have to make serious modifications to strengthen the engine (forged pistons, aftermarket connecting rods, etc.).

Your engine's existing compression ratio is a factor in how much boost you can run. Ratios are high in most Focus applications. To make lots of boost (over 10 psi) your static compression ratio shouldn't be higher than about 9:1. Racers with on-the-edge turbo or supercharger setups start with 7:1 compression with forged pistons.

Heat and detonation

Knock, ping, pre-ignition and detonation are all terms that describe abnormal combustion in an engine - they also describe big trouble. An increase in boost also increases the combustion chamber temperature and pressure, often leading to these problems that can destroy pistons, valves, rods and crankshafts.

The two main factors in detonation and its control are heat and timing. Ignition timing does offer some ways to deal with detonation. Supercharged

Good for any forced induction application, Holley makes this boost-compensating adjustable fuel pressure regulator – adjustment range is from 20 to 75 psi and it will raise fuel pressure four psi for each psi of boost the engine sees

If you need to have a stronger head gasket to handle boost, this GReddy metal-reinforced piece is what you need – some are available in a thick version to reduce static compression so you can apply more boost

You need more power than just adding a blower? ATI built this outrageous Focus powered by a four-cam Ford modular V8 with SVT supercharger – V8 kits and rear-drive conversions are available from Kugel Komponents

This shot of the JR Focus kit outside the car shows how the long belt arrangement works the blower drive in with all the factory accessories

engines generally "like" more timing, especially initial advance, but once you are making full boost and the vehicle is under load, too much ignition advance can bring on the "death rattle" of detonation that you don't want to hear. How much advance your application can handle is a trial-error-experience thing, but if you are using a production blower kit from a known manufacturer, these tests have already been made and some kind of timing control program should be included.

Anything you can do to control engine temperature and intake air temperature in particular will help stave off detonation also. Better oil circulation, a better radiator, an intercooler and an engine oil cooler are proven modifications to control excess heat that can contribute to detonation.

Blower kits

There are several types of small superchargers used in kits designed for Focus engines. The two main types of supercharger design you will see are the Roots type or "positive displacement," and the centrifugal design.

The Roots-type mechanical blower uses a pair of rotors that turn inside a housing. As the rotors turn, they capture a certain amount of air and propel it to the inner circumference of the case and out to the intake manifold. Each time they turn around, they capture air, hence the "positive" description. The benefit of this type is that it starts making boost at very low rpm.

A variation of this type of blower is the screw-type. These have two rotors with helically-wound vanes that, as the name implies, look like two giant screws. When the two screws mesh together, the air is actually compressed between the screws.

The other major type of bolt-on supercharger is the centrifugal design. From a quick examination, the centrifugal blower looks just like the compressor half of a turbocharger, being a multi-vaned wheel within a scroll-type housing. Unlike a turbocharger, this type of blower isn't driven by exhaust but by a mechanical drive from the engine, usually a belt. These types of blowers are not "positive-displacement," and thus do not necessarily make their boost down on the low end, but have plenty of air-movement potential when they are spinning rapidly.

Most reputable blower kits have everything you need to install the system and use it reliably. Contents include the blower, intake manifold (if needed), belt, mounting hardware, instructions and some type of electronic gear to control fuel delivery and/or ignition timing. Some kits use a larger-than-stock fuel pump that replaces your in-tank pump, and a special fuel pressure regulator that may be boost-sensitive.

Other included components could be hoses, wire harnesses, air intake, a new MAP sensor that can tolerate pressure as well as vacuum, an intercooler, and parts that relocate items in the engine compartment to provide room for the blower.

The serious nitrous-equipped Focus has improvements in the ignition system, exhaust header and cold-air intake – the addition of the supercharger on this one just makes it more of a "rice-crusher"

Nitrous Oxide

Nitrous oxide as a horsepower source can appear to be a miracle or a curse, depending on your experience. It's a fact that nitrous oxide (N2O) is the simplest, quickest and cheapest way to gain a large horsepower boost in your car. It's often referred to as the "liquid supercharger." But, just like in children's fairy tales, you court disaster if you don't follow the rules that come with the magic potion.

Nitrous oxide is an odorless, colorless gas that doesn't actually burn. It carries oxygen that allows your engine to burn extra fuel. When you inject nitrous oxide and gasoline at the same time in the proper proportions at full throttle, you'll get a kick in the butt as if you were instantly driving a car with an engine twice as big!

Done right, a nitrous kit is one of the best horsepower-per-dollar investments you can make, and is the most popular power-adder for small engines. Kits are available that add from 50 hp to 300 hp, because the more nitrous and fuel you add, the more power the engine makes . . . right up to the point where the engine comes apart. In the end, it is the durability of the engine itself that determines how much nitrous you can run. As tempting as it is to just keep putting bigger nitrous jets in your engine for more power, you need to do your research first to find the limits of your engine and what can be done to protect against damage done by a little too much nitrous fun.

The serious drag racers have done everything possible to their engines to strengthen them to handle big loads of nitrous. At a very minimum, you'll need to assure adequate fuel flow (of high-octane fuel) and probably retard the ignition timing. Many racers use electronic retard boxes that allow you to retard the ignition timing from the driver's seat. Usually, you'll need to put in a more capable ignition system than the stock one (with colder spark plugs), and it's wise to add a low-fuel-pressure shut-off switch - this device will save your engine if your fuel pressure ever drops too low while you're "on the bottle."

> **Warning:**
> Nitrous oxide is an oxidizer stored under pressure, and therefore potentially flammable and dangerous. Make sure the bottle is in a safe place and that all connections are secure, conforming to all applicable safety standards. Check with the manufacturer of your nitrous kit for more information. Also check with local authorities concerning any applicable laws.

Your nitrous is generally stored in a 10-pound metal bottle mounted in the trunk – it should be kept out of direct sun and mounted with the knob end forward, the label up and the bottle tilted slightly up at the front as shown here

This complete Focus nitrous kit from NOS (Holley) comes with unique plate-style injection and an rpm "window" switch to prevent rpm-induced backfires from the factory rev limiter

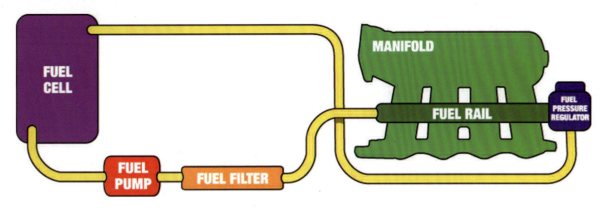

Typical EFI fuel system, as used with a "dry" nitrous system (Courtesy of Edelbrock Corp.)

No laughing matter

Nitrous can be intoxicating, but confine your high to the feeling you get from gobs of extra horsepower, not from inhaling the nitrous. Yes, it was once called "laughing gas" and used by dentists as an anaesthetic, but that is medical-grade nitrous, which is a controlled substance. What you're going to buy at your local tuner or speed shop is industrial-grade nitrous, which has a serious irritant added to it. If you try to inhale this stuff, you'll be sorry. Your engine, on the other hand, will love it.

If you're going to push much past a 60-horsepower system, and certainly if you're into the 100 horsepower-and-up category, you'll need to consider internal engine upgrades to handle the additional horsepower. Generally, forged pistons are used with these higher-horsepower kits, and most stock engines generally do not have performance-style forged pistons. So, if you're planning to have your engine live very long at these high-horsepower levels, you'll need to spend some money upgrading the "bottom end" of the engine.

Nitrous kits

The basic street-use nitrous kit consists of: a nitrous bottle, usually one that holds 10 pounds of liquid nitrous oxide; bottle mounting brackets and hardware; fuel and nitrous jets; high pressure lines, usually braided-stainless-covered AN-type with a Teflon inner liner for the high nitrous pressure; nitrous filter; solenoids, switch and electrical connectors. Kits are always sold without the nitrous in the bottle; you'll have to go to a local speed shop to have the bottle filled

There are two basic types of nitrous kits that differ in how the nitrous and fuel are delivered; the "dry" system and the "wet" system. The "dry" system has a nozzle and solenoid only for the nitrous, and this nozzle may be almost anywhere in the intake system; behind the MAF (Mass Air Flow) sensor (if equipped) and ahead of the throttle body is typical. The dry systems are designed for factory fuel-injected engines. To deliver the extra fuel to go with the nitrous, the stock system fuel pressure is raised during the WOT (wide-open throttle) period of nitrous usage, and reverts back to the stock fuel pressure in all other driving conditions.

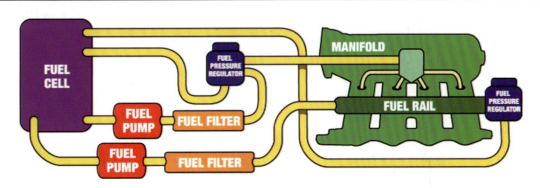

Typical EFI fuel system, as used with the "wet" nitrous setup (Courtesy of Edelbrock Corp.)

The two-piece construction of the Focus intake manifold lends itself to the plate system – the plate that adds the nitrous and extra fuel sandwiches between the two manifold halves

In "wet" systems, the nitrous nozzle (arrow) can mix and spray both gasoline and nitrous into the intake – separate solenoids control the flow of each power-adding half of the mix

The "wet" nitrous systems have solenoids for both nitrous and fuel, both of which are turned on when the nitrous system is activated. The fuel and nitrous in a simple system are plumbed into a single injector that merges the two, the gasoline and its oxidizer, as they enter the engine. More sophisticated wet systems may have a nitrous nozzle for each cylinder of the engine, and one or more fuel nozzles mounted separately. In high-output racing applications, individually feeding each cylinder allows for tuning each cylinder separately for fine control. The extra nozzles also mean there is ample supply of nitrous and fuel for very high-horsepower installations.

There are all sorts of "bells and whistles" available as extra features on most of the nitrous kits on the market today. There are varying designs of nozzles, different electronic controls that work with your factory computer to control timing and fuel delivery, optional bottle covers, bottle warmers, remote shut-off valves for the bottle, PCM piggybacks that pull back the ignition timing under nitrous use, and "staged" nitrous kits that deliver a certain amount during launch, then a little more, and the full blast for the top end.

How does it work?

In basic terms for a simple nitrous system, the tank or bottle of nitrous oxide is mounted in the trunk and plumbed up to the engine compartment with a high-pressure line. This is connected to an electric solenoid, from which nitrous (still a liquid at this point) can flow to the nozzle attached to your intake system. If you turn on an "arming" switch in the car, battery voltage is available to another switch that is located on your throttle linkage such that it is switched only when your right foot gets to "wide open throttle". Nitrous must only be injected at wide-open throttle.

Flip the arming switch and when you're hard on the throttle the solenoid releases nitrous oxide, which passes through a sized jet or orifice and turns into a vapor, to mix with your vaporized fuel in the engine. The extra fuel admitted at the same time as the N2O is easily oxidized and creates enough cylinder pressure to add 50, 75, 100 or more horsepower in an instant. So, do some research, talk to some tuners and then decide if going on the bottle is the right choice for you.

There are a variety of aftermarket ignition and fuel "modules" designed to electronically alter the spark and fuel curves under conditions such as boost or nitrous – for drag racing, this NOS controller can be programmed for several stages of nitrous application – the big shot comes only after the vehicle has full traction on the strip

Above: The most universal sport compact kit from Nitrous Express is this one that is adjustable from 35-50-75 horsepower levels – this wet-style kit needs no electronics for timing retard and uses the stock fuel pump

Left: The N2O solenoids and controls should be mounted in the engine compartment, close to the intake system – this installation is a hot street performer with nitrous *and* a supercharger

The typical sport compact engine compartment has had some modifications to the engine – usually to the "in-and-out" sides like a performance exhaust header and a cold ram-air intake for improved sound, looks and breathing power

Induction systems

Performance air intakes are available in two basic forms: the "short ram" and the "cold air" intake. In each case the idea is to get more - and colder - air into your engine. Looks are important, too, and nobody opens their hood unless they at least have a short ram.

The least expensive and easiest intakes to install are the short ram types. You'll spend more time getting the stock air filter box and inlet tube out than installing the short ram. If you have any doubts about removing the stock components, consult the Haynes repair manual for your car. Short ram intakes place the new filter relatively close to the engine, and modifications to the engine or body are rarely necessary. Most short ram installations take only a half-hour to install and may be good for 4 to 8 horsepower, depending on the application. And of course, they look and sound really nice. The more free-flowing they are, the more intake noise you'll hear in the car, but that's OK with us, right?

For purposes of performance, the colder the air the more power you make. Cold air intake systems are one of the most-widely-installed bolt-on performance improvements in the sport compact world. They are usually the first modification made to an engine, and have become so common that people want one on their car whether

The simplest modification you can make to your stock air induction system is to open the factory airbox, lift out the OEM paper air filter, and replace it with a high-flow aftermarket filter with a pleated-cotton lifetime filter - these can be reused over and over by washing them, then treating them with a special oil

For a little more power than the short rams offer, you can install a long ram like this AEM unit that picks up air below the fender on a Focus – note how the MAF sensor bolts to the new tube with no change in wiring

To protect your engine against ingesting rainwater, the AEM bypass valve pulls air through an external diaphragm to keep dry air flowing, even if the filter is clogged with water - such valves can generally be used only on normally-aspirated (not supercharged or turbocharged) applications

it makes any more power or not. The long ram intakes pick up air from down below the car's bumper or in the fenderwell, where the air is coolest (not so affected by engine heat), hence the long ram kits are usually called CAI's for Cold Air Intake.

If there's a drawback to the longer CAI, it's the possibility that the filter end of the tube could pick up water when driving in the rain, which could seriously damage your engine. Some companies offer rain hoods for the air pickup, and a relief valve can also be used to prevent water getting all the way through the intake system.

Aftermarket cold air intake systems can be worth 8 to 20 horsepower, depending on the design and how modified the engine is. A stock engine doesn't need to gulp and huge quantities of air, but a modified engine does. Obviously, a cold air intake is going to need some bends in order to reach the cold air, but if there are too many bends or bends made too sharp, the horsepower gain from the colder air could be offset by a reduction in airflow.

The rest of your induction system will be fine unless you're making bigger engine modifications, such as hotter cam(s), cylinder head work, increased compression and/or power adders like a blower or nitrous oxide. When you're really going for all you can get from your Focus engine, you can add a bigger throttle body and a high-flowing aftermarket intake manifold to really perform at high rpm. Just remember that modifying your engine to run its best at high rpm means it isn't going to be so hot anymore at low, around-town speeds, and throttle response can get seriously "doggy" unless you're constantly blipping the right foot pedal.

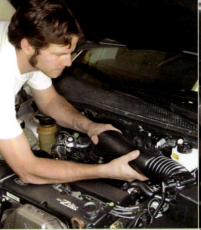
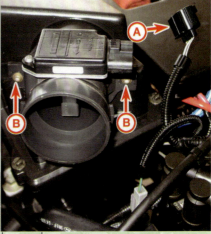

01 FocusSport makes this "Cool-Flow" intake that utilizes a high-performance cone-type air filter that is kept behind a metal "dam" to keep the hot engine compartment air from getting to the engine's air intake, they also make a longer "race" CAI of metal tubing that goes below the car for cool air

02 Disconnect the battery, then begin by removing the clamps on the stock Focus air tube at the throttle body (engine side) and at the other end where it connects to the MAF (Mass Air Flow) sensor at the filter box - remove the air tube

03 Disconnect the electrical connector (A) from the MAF sensor, then remove the two Torx screws (B) that secure the MAF to the filter box – remove the MAF and handle it carefully

Fresher breath for your Focus!

04 Disconnect the crankcase ventilation hose from the filter box and the valve cover and remove the hose

05 You can remove the filter box by rocking it a little, then pulling it straight up – it's retained in the car only by pins on the bottom that fit into rubber grommets

06 With the filter box removed, you have access to remove these two nuts

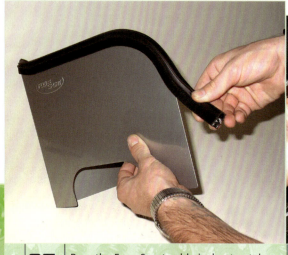

07 Prep the FocusSport cold air sheetmetal "dam" by pressing the sealing strip around the edges

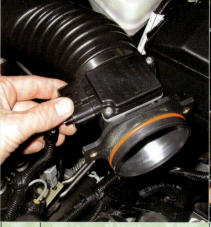

08 Reinstall the air tube at the throttle body, connect the electrical connector to the MAF sensor, then insert the MAF sensor into the air tube, but don't fully tighten the clamp at this time

09 Install the sheetmetal dam by bolting it down with the two nuts removed in Step 6 – here the MAF sensor is aligned with its mounting hole in the dam

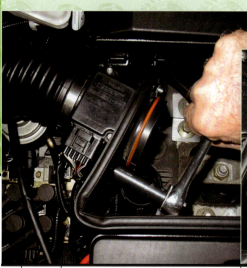

13 Now bolt the MAF sensor to the dam and we're almost done

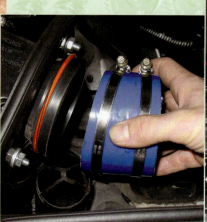

14 Push the new silicone hose over the protruding end of the MAF sensor, with the hose at about this angle, and tighten the clamp at the MAF sensor end

15 Place the new cone-style performance filter into the new blue hose and secure the hose clamp there

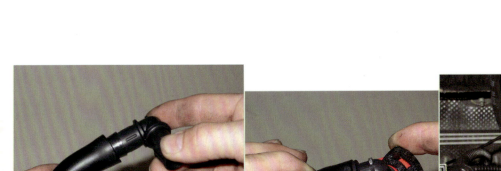

10 Take your crankcase ventilation hose and cut it about in half, then insert the plastic elbow in one end

11 Slip the new FocusSport crankcase ventilation filter onto the elbow, then secure it by squeezing the clamp

12 Push the other end of the vent hose back onto the valve cover fitting

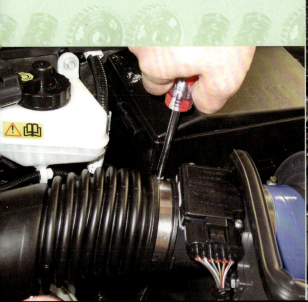

16 Now's the time to go back and make sure all hose clamps are secured

17 Here's the finished installation – you can see how when the hood is closed hot engine air is kept out, while the filter gets fresh air only from the original ducting in the body (below where the old filter box was)

Engine performance

Computers and chips

The engine computers in our modern vehicles were developed to make cars more fuel-efficient and emissions clean, using computer-controlled electronic fuel injection. The side benefit for performance enthusiasts is that engine control modifications to the fuel and ignition systems are relatively easy.

For a minimal outlay of cash and trouble, a simple chip upgrade for your PCM can improve engine response with increased timing – to go along with this, you may have to upgrade the octane of your fuel to premium, especially if your engine has high compression – this is a "plug-and-play" chip for the Focus from DiabloSport

Engine management basics

Automotive computer systems consist of an onboard computer, referred to by Ford as the Powertrain Control Module (PCM), and information sensors, which monitor various functions of the engine and send data to the PCM. Based on the data and the information programmed into the computer's memory, the PCM generates output signals to control various engine functions via control relays, solenoids and other output actuators.

The PCM is the "brain" of the electronically controlled fuel and emissions system, and is specifically calibrated to optimize the performance, emissions, fuel economy and driveability of one specific vehicle/engine/transaxle/accessories package in one make/model/year of vehicle.

Not all PCM's have a customer-serviceable chip, but computer upgrade work can be done by mail – Jet Performance Products can do upgrades for most sport compact PCM's and ship it back to you in 24 hours, all with the special packaging they will supply you

"Non-serviceable" chips must be carefully unsoldered from the board, which is why this is usually done by a specialized company or tuning shop with the proper tools and reprogramming equipment

Computer codes keep track

You may have heard of the term OBD or OBD-II. This means On-Board Diagnostics and refers to the ability to retrieve information from the PCM about the performance characteristics and running condition of all the sensors and actuators in the engine management system. This is invaluable information in diagnosing engine problems. The PCM will illuminate the CHECK ENGINE light (also called the Malfunction Indicator Light) on the dash if it recognizes a component fault.

So, if your dashboard warning light comes on you know the computer has spotted something it doesn't like. To then figure out what it has found, you (or your mechanic) need to access the diagnostic code that the computer has stored in its memory for that fault. On some vehicles, getting these codes is an easy in-the-driveway job. On others, it takes an expensive "scan tool." Your Haynes repair manual will give specific information for your make and model.

Add-on chips and computers

For improved performance, many enthusiasts upgrade their computer chips, or replace their entire computer. The advantages are increased fuel flow, an improved ignition advance curve and higher revving capability. While replacing computer components can provide substantial performance gains when combined with other engine upgrades, they also have their downside. Perhaps most importantly, replacing any original-equipment computer components can void your warranty or cause you to fail an emissions inspection. Nevertheless, if you are seriously into modifying your engine, at some point you will have to consider dealing with the computer.

The factory programming in your car's PCM is a highly developed, extensively-tested system that works perfectly for your engine in stock condition. Remember that the goal of the factory engineers is maximum fuel economy, driveability, longevity and efficiency. Our goals as enthusiasts are more in the high-performance sphere and our programming needs are slightly different. The average person driving an import car will never see 6000 rpm in the car's lifetime, but the average enthusiast wants to see the upper power band as often as possible.

Where the factory PCM programming needs some "help" for performance use is in the ignition timing and fuel curves. Virtually all new cars are designed to run on the lowest grade of unleaded pump gas, with an 87-octane rating. To get more performance, the ignition curve can be given more timing and the fuel curve adjusted for more fuel at

Before you order a custom chip for your Focus PCM, you must copy all the information from the label on your PCM, so the techs know exactly what Ford program and spark/fuel parameters they're working with

higher rpms, but the octane rating of the gas now becomes a problem. When more timing is added, the engine may have more tendency to exhibit detonation or ping, signs of improper burning in the combustion chamber and potentially dangerous to the lifespan of the engine. Thus, if you want more timing in your computer for more power, you'll probably have to up the grade of gasoline you buy. In fact, the more serious engine modifications you make, the more you will probably have to "reprogram" your PCM.

While most bolt-on engine modifications will work well with increased timing, the serious "power adders" like nitrous oxide, superchargers, turbochargers and even just high-compression pistons will require less ignition advance. The big gains in horsepower come from modifications that increase the cylinder pressure in the engine, the force pushing the pistons down. Increases in cylinder pressure really raise the octane requirement in a hurry. The best you can get at most gas stations won't be enough to stave off detonation, unless you're lucky enough to live near one of the few stations that sells 100-octane unleaded "racing" gas, and that gets pricey.

So, over the process of modifying your Focus' engine, your programming needs may change. As you make more and different changes, different tweaks need to be applied to the "brain." Hopefully, you have located a trustworthy "tuning" shop near you. They'll be able to help you with computer upgrades.

In many new cars, the programming that affects the areas we want to modify is part of a "chip" on the motherboard of the PCM. The chip is a very small piece of silicon semiconductor material carrying many integrated circuits. These are usually called PROM chips, for Programmable Read Only Memory. In some cases, the chip is a "plug-in" which can be easily removed from the PCM and replaced with a custom chip. Other chips are factory-soldered to the board. Cars with plug-in chips are the easiest to modify, but many imports do not have replaceable chips.

It isn't recommended to remove a soldered chip from the motherboard at home. Your factory PCM is very expensive to replace and just a small mistake with the solder or the heat source could ruin it. Aftermarket companies offer reprogramming services for these kinds of PCM's, and some tuning shops also have equipment to do this. In most cases you remove your PCM and send it to the company by overnight mail, they modify it and overnight-mail it back to you. Luckily for Focus owners, the chip in the PCM is a do-it-yourself project that only takes about 45 minutes.

Based on the information you have given them about your vehicle, driving needs, and modifications you have made to the engine, they will custom-program the timing, fuel and even the transmission shifting information on vehicles with PCM-controlled electronic automatic transaxles. On vehicles so equipped, they can even change the factory-set rev limiter. On most applications, your car will require a better grade of gas than before, so factor the increased fuel cost in your budget.

01 This is the location of the PCM in your Focus – the glove box is lowered down here for clarity but does not have to be removed for accessing the computer

Performance "chipping" the Focus

06 If you get your chip from your DiabloSport, it will have been customized for your car and comes with complete instructions, cleaning supplies and other information about tuning

02 You do have to remove the right kick panel to access the PCM – just use a trim tool to pop out the plastic pins, then twist the kick panel out – CAUTION: You must disconnect the battery before going any further

03 Now you can see the bottom of the PCM – remove the bolt and the plastic cover over the electrical connectors, then carefully remove the connectors – pull them straight off, don't twist them

04 The PCM is actually retained by clips in the body, so at this point you can just pull the PCM downward to remove it from the car

05 Remove this black plastic dust cover and you can see the metal contact that the new chip will install onto

07 Use the small Scotch-Brite pad supplied to clean the top and bottom surfaces of the metal contact – a good connection here is vital

08 DiabloSport also supplies a swab and cleaning solution to do the final cleanup on the PCM contacts

09 Now you can slide the DiabloSport chip in until it goes over the PCM contacts

10 Reinstall the black plastic cap, then use the DiabloSport stick-on covering to further protect the PCM from dust or moisture – put the PCM back in and you're ready for better performance and a higher rev-limit as well

An aftermarket coil with more windings and a heavy-duty case can up your secondary voltage to the spark plugs considerably – important if you plan to run high cylinder pressures in your engine like this supercharged Focus

Ignition system

Higher engine speeds put an increased load on stock ignition systems, but modifications that lead to increased cylinder pressure can really put out the fire. If you install higher-compression pistons - always a good move for increased engine performance - the spark plugs need a lot more zap to light off a mixture that is packed tighter than ever. The denser the mixture, the harder it is for a spark to jump the plug's electrodes, like swimming through wet concrete. Other major power-adders such as nitrous oxide, supercharging or turbocharging also create much higher cylinder pressures and require ignition improvements to handle this.

Aftermarket ignition coils

The typical aftermarket coil is capable of making more secondary voltage than the stock coil, so the spark can jump the gap even at extreme cylinder pressures. An aftermarket coil won't add any horsepower and won't improve your fuel economy, but it could eliminate some misfire problems in the upper rpm range, and that will become more important as you add other modifications to your engine. The Focus doesn't have a conventional distributor to divvy out the sparks to each cylinder, but rather a coil pack that contains several coils, each controlled and timed by the car's computer (PCM as it is usually called). Simple kits are available to add a more powerful, aftermarket coil pack to the Focus ignition system.

Plug Wires

Aside from making your engine compartment look cool, high performance spark plug wires serve a very useful purpose. If you install a high-voltage coil and keep your stock wires, you are asking for voltage to leak from the wires under load, at high engine speeds, or boosted (blown or turbocharged) conditions. Voltage will try to seek the "path of least resistance" and that could be any engine ground that is close to one of your plug wires.

The typical factory plug wire has a core of carbon-impregnated material surrounded by fiberglass and rubber insulation, which is fine for stock engines.

Most aftermarket performance wires use a very fine spiral wire wound around a magnetic core and wrapped in silicone jacketing, and are available in thicker-than-stock diameters to handle more current flow. Some sport compact cars have stock plug wires as skinny as 5 or 6mm, while aftermarket wires are offered in 8mm, 8.5mm and even 9mm for racing applications. Good aftermarket wires also come with thicker boots, which is important, since the boot-to-plug contact area is a frequent source of voltage leaking to ground. Wires in the 8mm range are big enough to handle the spark of most street-modified cars, and the bigger wires are good for racing, but there's no such thing as having too much insulation on your plug wires.

> **Warning:** Carbon-conductor wires have a very fragile core. Never try to bend them sharply or pull on them.

Your Focus is probably already in need of new plug wires, so go for a set of fatter and more colorful performance wires that look good and can handle your high rpm usage without voltage leaks

Timing controls

Once you start modifying the engine, you have changed the ignition parameters and you now need to adjust the timing with something other than the factory PCM. Installing a chip or reprogramming your PCM will advance the timing, but can't increase the energy level of the spark. For that you need a CD (Capacitive Discharge) aftermarket ignition system.

The CD ignition usually consists of an electronic box you mount in the engine compartment, and the wiring harness to connect to your vehicle. Your PCM still does the triggering and controls the advance, but in the CD box is a large capacitor, which is an electronic storage device. These ignition systems have been used in performance applications for years and are well proven. Juice usually comes into the coil or coil pack as battery voltage (12V) and is bumped up from there to 5,000, 10,000 or 40,000 volts of secondary current. In the CD ignition, the capacitor stores incoming juice until there is more like 450 volts to go to the coil. Now the coil has a much easier time of quickly building up to the required voltage for good spark, regardless of the rpm.

> **Caution:** When removing spark plug wires, pull only on the boot. Never pull on the plug wire itself. The plug wire's core is fragile and can be broken by careless stretching.

An electronic ignition control box can provide multi-fire capability as well as user-settable control of rev-limit, plus retard control for boosted engines and nitrous applications

A multi-spark capacitive-discharge (CD) ignition like the Holley " Quick Strip Annihilator" is especially useful for modified engines – the box is fitted with EEPROM microprocessors that can be overwritten many times and adjusts the spark output based on engine rpm – there's even a "soft-touch" programmer keypad for racing

Spark plugs

The final links in the ignition system's chain-of-command are the spark plugs, the front-line combat troops. We may have mentioned this before but, as with other ignition modifications, don't expect to make big gains in power or mileage by switching spark plugs. Despite the wild claims dreamed up by advertising copywriters over the last fifty years, the only time spark plugs will make much difference on a street-driven engine is when the engine is really in need of a tune-up and you install fresh plugs.

Nonetheless, there are a wide variety of spark plugs out there to choose from. If your engine is only mildly modified, stick with the factory recommended spark plugs, gapped to factory specs. Most engines with above-average level of modifications can utilize a plug that is one heat range colder than stock.

Required Reading. . . your spark plugs!

Without a lot of complicated and expensive test equipment, you can tell a great deal about the operating conditions inside your engine just by examining its spark plugs.

This may seem like a primitive tuning tool, but watch the pit activity at any professional-level race and you'll see the top mechanics looking at spark plugs with a magnifying glass. When a spark plug tells a story, it can save you an entire engine by giving early warning signs of detonation. The color, uniformity, cleanliness and even smell of a freshly-pulled spark plug can tell you reams, if you know what to look for. In the back of the Haynes repair manual for your vehicle (you do have one, don't you?) you'll find a large chart of various spark plug conditions, close-up and in color.

When you pull the plugs on your street-driven machine, you're looking at long-term conditions - the plugs can tell you if the engine is too rich, too lean, if it's burning oil, if the electrodes are worn from too many miles, etc. At the race track conditions are quite different than everyday driving. When you're ready to make a run at the drags, install a fresh set of plugs and make your run, but just as you go through the lights, shut off the engine "clean" and put the trans in neutral at the same time (make sure you don't turn your ignition key to the LOCK position, or you won't be able to steer).

You may never have looked at a spark plug this closely, but you should know some of the plug terminology so you can discuss diagnostics with an experienced tuner

Coast back to the pits or have a friend tow you. Pull these plugs and you'll see only what plug conditions are the result of hard running *on that run only*. You must shut off clean, or the deceleration and pit driving could show a false richness or oil symptoms. If your plug is free of the signs of detonation, like pits or the presence of aluminum specks on the porcelain, then you're good to run hard.

Whenever you make important changes on your state of tune, like adding more performance equipment, doublecheck the part's influence by doing a plug check like this. Too rich, and you'll just go too slow. Too lean and you'll toast the engine if you're not careful. The simple plug check tells you if you're safe or not!

The condition of your spark plugs is a good indicator of conditions inside your engine – check your plugs after each new modification to see if you need to change fuel and/or timing calibrations

A really good close-up magnifying glass will let you see every tiny detail - compare the results to a Haynes color spark plug chart

Treat your Focus to a hot coil pack and new wires

01 Remove the spark plug wires from the coil pack, noting which wires go to which terminal (it would be a good idea to make a simple sketch)

02 To remove the factory coil pack, disconnect the ignition system electrical connector, then remove the coil pack mounting screws (see your Haynes Automotive Repair Manual, if necessary)

03 The new MSD performance coil pack is bigger than stock, and on some models like our project Focus, the coil pack must be spaced away from the factory bracket to clear – we found these aluminum spacer tubes and longer Allen screws at the hardware store

04 Secure the spacers to the coil bracket with a dab of RTV sealant just to hold them, then position the MSD coil pack and install the four new Allen screws

  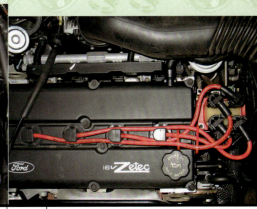

05 With the new coil pack secured, reinstall the ignition connector - pull the wire clip out, push on the connecter, then push the wire clip back in place

06 New performance wires are required to use the new MSD coil pack. To keep the correct firing order, refer to the sketch you made in Step 1. Make sure you push the end of each wire firmly into position

07 Here's the new coil pack all mounted and wired up with heavy-duty plug wires – our project Focus will now have the electrical fortitude to handle whatever power-adders we install later on

Engine performance

Valvetrain Modifications

When you run fast, you breathe harder - so does your engine. To make more power, an engine must "inhale" more air and "exhale" more exhaust. To make this happen, you can open the valves more, leave them open longer and/or enlarge the "ports" (passages in the cylinder head where the air and exhaust flow). These cylinder head and valvetrain modifications can seem complicated, but understanding them is essential. Mistakes here can cost you power or even an engine overhaul.

What happens when you override your factory rev-limiter at 8000 rpm with weak valve springs? – This valvehead imbedded in a piston is the typical result of valve float

If you make no other mod to your valvetrain, at least install quality performance valve springs and lightweight retainers like these from Crane – they could save your engine when you spend time at high revs

The modifications discussed here usually come after all the other bolt-ons have not gained you the power you're after. Most of these modifications require going inside the engine, which is not a place an amateur should go alone. You'll need to find a reputable tuner and machine shop who know your particular engine inside and out.

Cam sprockets

A cam gear or gears (more properly, sprockets) swap is a very popular modification on Overhead Cam (OHC) engines. They not only look great, they can actually provide a few extra horsepower when set up properly. While dialing in the degrees on the sprockets is relatively easy, you will need to know the precise number of degrees to advance or retard each cam in your particular application. The correct "degreeing in" specifications are determined by the engine type, level of modification and type of power you're after (low-rpm or high-rpm). Because of this complexity, it's best to ask a tuner who's familiar with your type of engine, or go by the recommendations that come with the gears.

Installing cam gears means you'll have to remove, then reinstall the timing belt. This procedure is best left to a qualified technician, since any slight error could cause you to bend your valves from valve-to-piston contact. At the very least, get the Haynes repair manual for your particular vehicle and follow the procedure carefully. Be sure to rotate the engine through two turns by hand after the belt is back on and double-check that all the timing marks are still aligned - this way you'll identify any problems before turning the key to the sound of grinding metal if you make a mistake.

You'll find that cam gears are one of the most popular engine modifications there is – adjustable cam timing gears like these from Kent Cams allow you to adjust camshaft timing to suit the other tuning modifications you have made or plan to

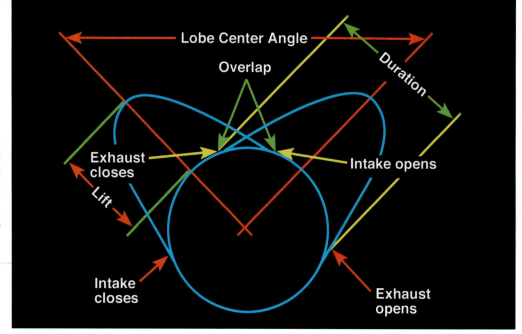

The relationship between camshaft intake and exhaust lobes is complicated and the right cam design can do wonders

Camshafts

Installing camshafts is an expensive and precise task. The most important work comes before any tools come out. You, consulting with your tuner, need to pick out the best cam for your car and driving style.

Stock camshafts are designed as a compromise to consider economy, emissions, low-end torque and good idling and driveability. The performance camshaft lifts the valves higher (lift), keeps them open longer (duration) and is designed mainly to produce more horsepower. A performance camshaft usually makes its gains at mid-to-higher rpm and sacrifices some low-rpm torque. The hotter the cam, the more pronounced these attributes become. A cam design that is advertised for power between 3000 and 8000 rpm won't start feeling really good until that rpm "band" is reached.

Aftermarket cams are usually offered in "Stages" of performance. A typical Stage 1 cam might have a little higher lift than stock and a little longer duration. It would still keep an excellent idle and work from idle or 1000 rpm up. A Stage II cam would be hotter in all specs (with a band from 3000 to 7000 rpm) and have a slightly rough idle (maybe 750 rpm). A Stage III cam would feature serious lift, duration and overlap and make its power from 5000 to 8000 rpm. The hotter the cam specs the worse the idle, low-end performance and fuel economy is going to be, but the more top-end horsepower you'll make.

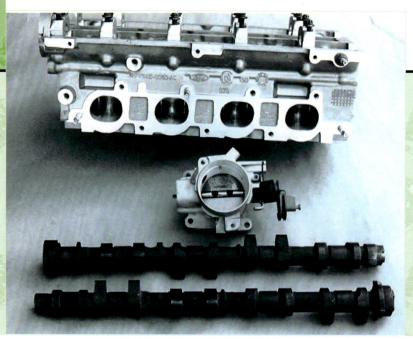

Gude calls this their "turbo-beater at half the price" – it's a Focus package that includes a ported cylinder head with performance cams that also includes a tweaked ECU and a bigger throttle body

The piston makes up half of the combustion chamber in a cylinder, and there are a number of choices when rebuilding an engine for performance – at left is a forged replacement piston with stock compression ratio, at center is a forging with very high compression for racing (note the high dome), and at right is the opposite end of the piston spectrum, a forged 8:1 dished piston for high-boost turbocharged applications

Valve springs

When you install a "bigger" camshaft, you'll usually want to install better valve springs. High-performance valve springs allow the valves to open further without the springs binding and also are stronger to prevent valve "float." Valve float occurs when the engine is at very high rpm and the inertia of the valve is too much for the spring to handle. So the valves actually lose contact with the lifter or cam follower and can make contact with the piston, bending the valve and/or damaging the piston.

For this reason, high-performance valve springs are recommended whenever you change the camshaft or make other modifications to extend the rpm range beyond stock. Your stock springs will not last long at repeated high-rpm operation, and when springs fail, the valves usually hit the pistons with results that are major-league bad.

Once you start altering the stock PCM or add an aftermarket controller that allows you to change the factory rev limit, it's only a matter of time before the stock valve springs in that 100,000-mile Focus you're starting with are going to fail.

When you are rebuilding your cylinder head, if you discover some bad valves, why not replace the whole set with performance valves that are lightweight and made of high-temp alloys to handle boosted and nitrous-equipped applications?

Cylinder head work

The most basic of cylinder head work is a valve job, which will assure the valve faces, seats and guides are in good condition. This is very important for an engine running at high rpm, and is essential if your engine has very many miles on it. If you're planning to install performance camshafts with new valve springs and lightweight retainers, make sure you get a good valve job at the same time, preferably a three-angle valve job from a performance machine shop. You won't see much performance gain from this work; it's insurance against damage on an engine that will be pushed to the limits.

Cylinder head porting is a specialized art and science that is practiced by performance machine shops. Novices can damage the cylinder head or actually reduce airflow. A performance machine shop has all the right equipment for the job, including a flow-bench. With the aid of a flow-bench, the performance machine shop can "open up" your heads for maximum performance. Be sure to find a shop that specializes in your type of engine.

The adjustable gear is two-piece, so the bolts can be loosened and the relationship between the inner section on the camshaft and the outer section connected to the timing belt can be advanced or retarded – Good ones are machined of billet aluminum and feature very clearly engraved timing marks

Engine performance

Fuel system

Your engine burns fuel and air. When you increase the amount of air it's using, you have to up the fuel, too. The more you modify your engine, the more fuel system modifications you may have to perform.

Holley offers billet fuel rails in four colors - they are available for either stock injectors or larger performance injectors

A performance-type adjustable fuel pressure regulator will be adequate for all your pressure control needs for now and with any future engine add-ons

Your stock engine management system will adapt to an increase in airflow such as an aftermarket intake pipe and free-flowing air filter, but the physical limitations of the stock fuel delivery system under wide-open throttle (WOT) conditions can hold back the engine's potential when more aggressive mods are made. Since you are modifying the engine to go faster, i.e. spending more time at WOT, you are sort of on your own to develop the fuel combination that works best for your engine and the modifications you've made. The major mods you might make, such as power-adders, cams or head work, have been done by many others before you, and the manufacturer of the components should have plenty of data on what fuel system upgrades go along with their equipment.

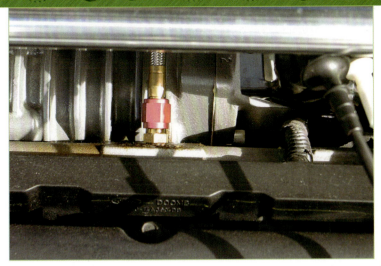

Here's a supercharged Focus with an aftermarket fuel rail that makes it easy to hook up an extra fuel line to feed an additional injector - these rails also accept cool-looking AN fittings and braided hoses

Tuning to find the correct air-fuel ratio when you're doing engine mods is a lot easier if you have a wide-band aftermarket oxygen sensor and gauge like this one from K&N that features ten LED lights in different colors that correspond to different A/F ratios

An aftermarket high-pressure fuel pump will be needed when you have serious power mods – some, like this one, replace your in-tank pump; other types can be added to the system somewhere near the fuel tank

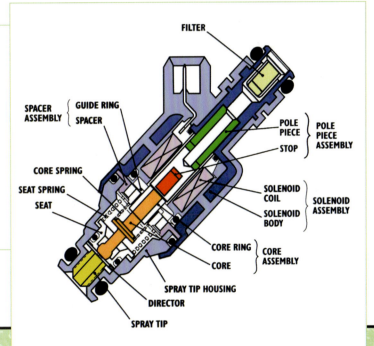

An electronic fuel injector is more complicated than you might think, so aftermarket performance injectors can be expensive - if you know you don't actually need bigger injectors, you can send your stock injectors to a company like RC Engineering and have them flow tested and balanced, protecting your engine from a burned piston due to one bad injector

An adjustable fuel pressure regulator is probably the first modification for your fuel system. The aftermarket units are a direct bolt-on replacement for the stock regulator, with the same vacuum connection, but feature an adjuster screw on top that changes the fuel system pressure. Once you start playing with your fuel system, you must have a reliable way to measure the fuel pressure, which usually means installing a quality fuel pressure gauge.

When you increase the fuel pressure in your FI system, you are putting a greater load on the injectors themselves. Experts tell us that for street cars with mild bolt-on modifications, you shouldn't raise the factory fuel pressure much more than 10% over stock. Engines built for all-out racing will require a completely aftermarket fuel system that delivers much higher pressure and volume, with special injectors, fuel pump, regulator, fuel rail and stand-alone engine management.

FWD traction is always limited, but especially so on regular streets – at the track, you've got all the hookup you can handle and you get some real competition – you don't have to get your times announced if you don't want that

Race and Live !

The basics

Street racing has been around a long time – today's legitimate organized drag racing was begun in the early 1950's as a reaction to hot rods racing on public streets.

But times have changed over the years. Now we have a huge increase in the number of very modified imports running around and at the same time, the number of deserted streets once deemed "safe enough" to race on have been eliminated by urban sprawl. Worse yet, the urban sprawl has led to the demise of many of the nation's race tracks.

The things that haven't changed about street racing is that the participants still get a thrill, racers and spectators still bet on the outcome of the matches and unfortunately, sometimes people get hurt or killed.

Even if no one is killed or hurt, there are serious negatives to street racing. Right now, the biggest weapon in the establishment's arsenal is vehicle confiscation. That means you lose your car forever. After all the hard work, investment and wrenching you've put into your modified sport compact, is this how you want it to end up?

In a number of areas where there is a legitimate race course or NHRA dragstrip, what local organizers have done is institute "street-legal" drags. On a Wednesday night, a Friday or some other day where the track doesn't have their professional program, the street racers come in for a nominal fee and make all the runs they want.

Such events have become very popular where they have been instituted. Racers and spectators can relax without fear of arrest, and the racers have the benefit of superior traction, guardrails, ambulance and firetruck on premises, and the chance to show off in front of much larger crowds of their peers. Like with the sports or music businesses, those who are good can advance up the ranks, make a name, build a true race car, and maybe one day be a sponsored touring professional drag racer like one of their heroes.

Race safe

There's no "bravery" in racing stupid - that is, without the basic safety items that can save your life or limbs. The good news is that any race-oriented safety device you add to your street-driven car only increases its cool factor, whether you race or not.

First off, you should really have a serious set of seat belts. Your factory shoulder belt is only OK. A wide-belt, racing harness is way better, both for safety and looks. Every time you strap in, you'll feel like one of the pro import racers! In most cases, such belts are installed in conjunction with an aftermarket seat, which is lighter and more rigid to keep you in place, especially if you ever decide to try some slalom or other road-course racing.

In the back seat area, carry around a legitimate (i.e. approved by NHRA or other sanctioning body) helmet. Have your name and blood type lettered on it just like the real racers do, and strap it to the back seat with a seat belt. It's always a conversation starter, and some tracks will make you get a helmet anyway.

The ultimate in safety and points-gathering is probably a roll-bar. You can buy bolt-in kits for a simple roll-bar for most popular imports, or have one bent and welded into the car at a race shop. It's not as expensive as you might think, and is way more impressive than neon lights under your car or a pod-mounted tach.

There are many more safety items of a technical nature that you can add to your ride, but we don't have space to detail all of them. Get yourself an NHRA rulebook, and do some research on the net. Most racetracks have a website with information on when they have street-legal drags or "grudge" nights. Also, look up *nhra.com*, *RaceLegal.com* (a San Diego group organizing events to get racers off the streets), and *racersagainststreetracing.com*. That last one is a coalition of aftermarket manufacturers, pro racers, car magazines and race sanctioning bodies dedicated to providing alternatives to street racing.

Try some real racing at a dragstrip, even if you go as a spectator the first time – at the import drags/street legal drags and other such grassroots events, you'll find lots of your peers having fun going fast and safe

A helmet, a set of firm racing seats and a racing harness will put some safety into your racing, plus look cool at any time - the chromed rollbar here just ups the safety/wow factor

In-car entertainment

09

DVD, Satellite radio, video screens in every headrest... isn't this a great world!

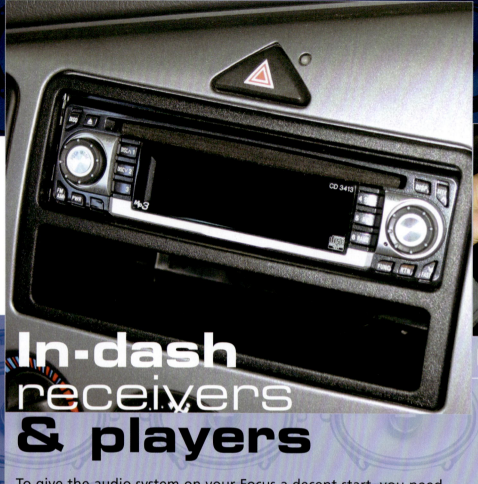

In-dash receivers & players

To give the audio system on your Focus a decent start, you need a good head unit to provide the signal that an amp will beef up, and that the speakers will replay.

If an upgrade of the sound system is what you have in mind, there are plenty of decent head units out there to choose from. Don't be afraid to consult with an expert on which features matter most. The head unit is an important part of a good sound system - always go for the best you can afford.

01 First, the old set's got to go. Resist the urge to just crowbar the thing out of the dash - you'll be needing two of the standard radio removal tools to do the job with less damage. And you could always sell it, or keep it, to stick back in when you sell the car.

05 The factory antenna needed an adapter plug so it could fit properly on the radio

06 A new cage was placed into the dash . . .

07 . . . and secured into place. Bending a few of the mounting tangs was all that was necessary

08 Next we connected the radio's harness connector and antenna . . .

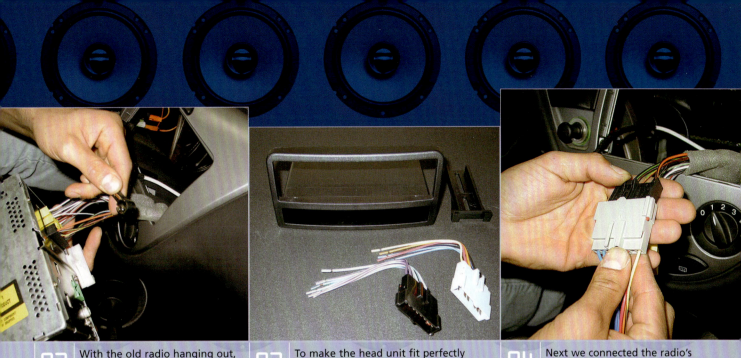

02 With the old radio hanging out, it was easy to disconnect the harness and antenna

03 To make the head unit fit perfectly in the dash, Scosche supplied us with a vehicle specific installation kit

04 Next we connected the radio's wiring harness to the factory harness connector

Our Eclipse head unit is typical of the current single-CD state of the art - nice appearance, good sound, plenty of features. The peak of in-car entertainment, so to speak.

09 ... then placed the radio into its cage. Push the radio home until it clicks. If it gets stuck, take the set out, and un-bunch all the wiring by hand. Do not force it in, or you could end up having a very bad day.

10 The installation kit was the last thing to do. A simple snap and our installation is complete. Success!

11 Now get out the instruction manual and set those levels properly. Enjoy!

9-3

Speakers

Most Focus factory speakers are low on power and made with nasty paper cones that disintegrate after a few years - installing any aftermarket speakers would be considered an upgrade. But we're going top-shelf with some really first-class speakers courtesy of our friends at JL Audio.

Crimp connectors

There is a wide variety of crimp-type connectors available at auto parts stores, which will allow you to make virtually any type of connection you need to make. To make the connections properly, you'll need to use a special crimping tool (available at most auto parts stores). Try to get a good-quality tool that presses an indentation into the connector. Some of the cheaper tools simply flatten the connector, which gives an inferior connection. Also, be sure you're using the correct connector type for the gauge of wire you're connecting.

If you don't know the wire gauge, you can figure it out using your crimping tool by inserting the end of the wire into each of the stripping holes in your crimper until you find the one that strips off the wire's insulation.

Crimp connectors are quick and easy to install - simply strip off about 1/4-inch of insulation using the proper-gauge hole on your stripping tool . . .

. . . insert the stripped wire and crimp the connector firmly onto it using the correct crimping jaws of the tool

Note:
When installing spade or bullet connectors, always crimp the female side of the connector to the feed wire. This way, if the connector comes unplugged, the "hot" wire won't short out if it touches a ground (it'll be shielded by the insulation surrounding the female side of the connector).

Wire gauge	Industry standard color on crimp connector
22 to 18	Red
16 to 14	Blue
12 to 10	Yellow

Front speakers

01 The best place for the front speakers is in the doors. Lucky for us the factory installed speakers were the same size, so a swap wasn't tuff at all. Off came the door panel. Don't just rip the panel off, be sure you've got all the screws out. Most door panels are also secured by push-in plastic fasteners around the perimeter of the panel (if necessary refer to the Haynes Automotive Repair Manual for your vehicle) . . .

02 . . . next came the ugly factory speaker

03 Once you've got the door trim panel off , and have removed the old speaker, it's time too think vibration. If you don't want all that kicking power to set your door panel trembling, you need to invest in some sound-deadening. Let's try Accumat by Scosche. Clean up the door panel with a decent cleaner . . .

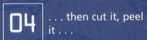

04 . . . then cut it, peel it . . .

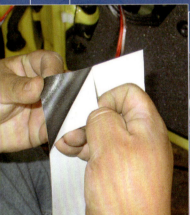

05 . . . and get it on. Don't get to carried away in your quest for sonic perfection, or you might find you've covered up some useful door features, like vital screw holes, or door trim panel clips. Trim round with a sharp knife to re-liberate your holes, etc.

06 Using a heat gun, heat the material slightly while applying pressure to the sheet so that the material conforms to the door's surface

07 If you're going for high-power front speakers, re-using the factory speaker wiring is not an option. Working new speaker wire through the doors electrical harness can't be done. Lucky for us, the A-pillar has an extra opening just below the doors harness

9-5

08 Feed the speaker wiring through at the bottom of the doors harness boot . . .

09 . . . then slip some heatshrink over the wires for protection

10 At the A-pillar remove the grommet, cut a small hole in it and feed the wire through the grommet and A-pillar. You only need to run enough speaker wire to just go under the dash, where the crossover is going to be mounted. Be sure to refit the grommet to prevent any water leaks

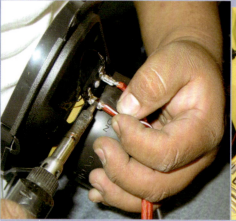

11 Carefully, solder the new wiring to the speaker and tweeter. If you don't feel comfortable with soldering, use proper speaker terminals

12 Being extremely careful that the drill doesn't slip and ruin your day (as well as your speakers), mount that speaker into place

13 Looks good! Oh, except for one thing . . .

14 . . . before replacing the door panel, remove that little trim ring that's taped to the speaker! Or else you'll be wondering why the speaker's got a rattle. (As you can see, we forgot.)

15 Check your set's instructions for connecting the crossovers, and how to mount them. Enjoy.

Rear speakers

01 The best place for the rear speakers in our ZX 3 is behind the rear quarter trim panel. Lucky for us the factory installed speakers are the same size, so the swap will be almost as easy as the front. We opted to remove the lower seat cushion. Not too difficult, just a few mounting bolts

02 One push pin and off comes the B-pillar panel, then a few clips and a little care, the same goes for the rear quarter panel (if necessary refer to the Haynes Automotive Repair Manual for your vehicle)

03 Four screws around front and a plug off the back, get that factory speaker out of here!

04 Before the speaker goes in, sound-deaden that tin. A piece of Accumat around the speaker holes should help. Either cut the speaker hole out completely, or slice across like a pizza and fold it in

05 Carefully, solder the new wiring to the speaker and tweeter. Once again, if you don't feel comfortable with soldering, use proper speaker terminals. Mount the speaker in place

06 That looks so much better - let's hope they sound as good as they look

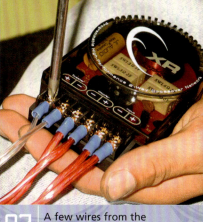

07 A few wires from the amp, and a few wires to the speaker (Check your set's instructions for connecting the crossovers). Use some good double-sided tape and secure that crossover to the inside panel. Good job!

Crossovers

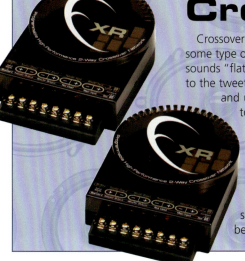

Crossovers separate different frequency bands and redirect them to the proper drivers. Without some type of crossover, these ranges of sound can't be separated, resulting in an audio system that sounds "flat" and/or distorted. So, they're incorporated into the system to send the high frequencies to the tweeters, mid-range frequencies to the mid-range speakers, low frequencies to the woofers, and ultra-low frequencies to the subwoofer(s), if used. Some are adjustable and can be set to separate these ranges at certain frequencies, thereby eliminating the frequencies that the speaker can't use (or that would cause it to operate inefficiently). Others aren't adjustable, and some are built right into a component (like a triaxial speaker).

There are two types of crossovers: active and passive. Active crossovers are placed into the signal chain before the amplifier, and require a separate DC voltage input to operate. Some amplifiers have built-in active crossovers.

Passive crossovers are placed into the signal chain between the amplifier and the speakers. They don't require DC voltage to operate. And, since they are connected just before the speakers, one amplifier can drive a number of speakers correctly.

9-7

Amplifiers

If you really want your sound system to crank, there's no substitute for power. And that means adding an amp.

Decide where you'll mount the amp carefully. Amps must be adequately cooled - don't cover it up so there's no airflow, and don't hang it upside down. We found ourselves a nice mounting platform under the passenger's seat.

TIP *Decide where you'll mount the amp carefully. Amps must be adequately cooled - don't cover it up so there's no airflow, and don't hang it upside down. We found ourselves a nice mounting platform under the front passenger's seat.*

01 First we removed the front seat. A simple matter of removing the four bolts securing the seat to the floorpan and lifting the seat from the vehicle. You may also have to disconnect an electrical connector or two. If your vehicle is equipped with side-impact airbags, you'll have to disable the airbag system (refer to the Haynes Automotive Repair Manual for your vehicle)

06 Cut a short length of wire for the ground and crimp a ring terminal on one end, then find a spot and mount it to the vehicle chassis. Be sure to sand off any paint so that the connection is made directly to metal

07 Read the amp's instruction book carefully when connecting any wires, or you might regret it. Identify your speaker positive and negative/ left side and right side wires, then make the connections. Securely connect the remote turn on wire, ground wire, and power cable to the amp

08 Time those RCA leads went on. Not much to this, just make sure not to mix them up (keep them the same as the connections made at the headset). If the cables were marked as previously mentioned, this shouldn't be a problem

09 With the installation complete it's time to install the fuse and test the amplifier. Carefully follow the manufacturer's instructions for powering up the amp and making any necessary adjustments

  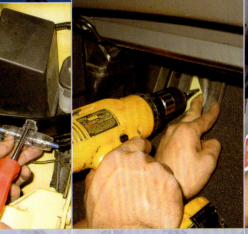

02 An amplifier wiring kit like this one from Scosche, supplies us with all our amplifier wiring needs

03 Running the amplifier's power wire starts at the battery. The main power wire needs to have a waterproof fuse holder mounted as close to the battery as possible. Connecting the power wire at the terminal is ok, just be sure NOT to install a fuse and complete the power connection until you finish the entire installation

04 The next step was deciding where best to run the power wire into the car, try and go for the most direct route. Here we see our installer carefully making a new hole on the passenger side floorboard. We used a grommet that came with the amplifier wiring kit to prevent any sharp edges from damaging the wire. Split loom was added for extra protection

05 The amplifier's remote turn on wire and signal patch cables need to be connected at the back of the stereo head. Marking the signal cables (left/right, front/rear) will assure correct connection at the amplifier

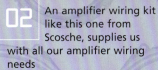 **Note:** Always follow the manufacturer's recommendations for mounting the amplifier. Properly securing an amp is very important so that it's not sliding around. A sliding amplifier that's not properly mounted can damage the unit, or worse, be dangerous in an accident.

Choosing the right amp

The first step is to determine the needs of your system. If you're just adding an amp to improve your original equipment system, you may need only minimal amplification. Therefore, a small inexpensive amp will suffice. On the other hand, if you're planning on running multiple subwoofers and component speakers, you'll most likely need multiple amplifiers.

Next, you have to figure out if you need an amplifier with a built-in crossover or an amp that is dedicated to playing a full-range signal. A built-in crossover can cross over different frequencies dedicated to a particular speaker, whereas a 12-inch subwoofer will sound best playing 100Hz and down. This will maximize the life of the speaker playing in this frequency range.

How powerful of an amp does your system need? Well, that depends what kind and how many speakers it has to drive. The amp should be capable of putting out 1-1/2 to two times the power (continuous, or RMS power in watts) that the lowest-frequency speaker that it'll be driving is rated. The specifications you'll find when shopping for an amp will indicate how many watts-per-channel the amp is able to produce continuously. This sounds weird, but an underpowered amp can actually damage your speakers when the volume is turned way up. The waveform it puts out changes from a nice curvy sine wave into more of a square wave, which speakers don't like; this is called clipping, because the top and bottom of the wave gets "clipped" off. The speakers can handle the extra power better than they can this ugly square wave.

Finally, how many channels must the amplifier have in order to interface with the stereo system? Say, for example, you're running four speakers and you want to add amplifiers to enhance the sound. You must decide if you want to retain the use of the fader. If you do, you will need to purchase a four-channel amplifier with four independent RCA inputs. A four-channel amplifier can run four speakers in a stereo fashion without losing fading capability.

Subwoofer

Want to actually *feel* the music pumping through your system?

Subwoofers are usually sold as a stand-alone item, but in just about all applications they will have to be mounted in some type of enclosure. These are big, heavy speakers that just can't be tossed into a door panel or under the dash. There are many types of enclosures, designed to manipulate the acoustics of the subwoofer(s) depending on the type of vehicle in which it is being installed or the type of music that will be listened to. The physics behind these various designs is not easy to understand and is way beyond the scope of this manual, so we won't go there. However, your basic choices are a ready-made cabinet, an enclosure that has been designed to replace a center console or side panel specifically for your model car, or a custom built enclosure you build yourself.

Ready-made cabinet

01 The wiring was already connected to the terminal cup that was fitted on the box, so the ends just needed stripping back and terminating with the correct fittings to join onto the subwoofer. The cable is coded with plus and minus symbols for easy connection. As long as you get the feed wire into the box the right way, everything will be fine

02 After carefully positioning the subwoofer to get the center logo straight, the eight mounting holes were drilled with pilot holes, and then the screws were tightened steadily by hand. You can use a power screwdriver, but be careful not to go too tight and ruin the pilot hole you've just drilled or you'll have to put your speaker in at a funny angle once you've drilled some more holes

03 The sub cable from the amplifier was clamped tightly under these screw terminals. Like the rest of the wiring, the cable was stripped back and then the ends protected with a short piece of heatshrink tube. This neatens the cable ends and makes it more difficult to short out the wiring. Just be sure to leave enough bare cable to connect to the terminal, eh?

Model specific enclosures

A slick option for adding a subwoofer is one of these ready-made vehicle-specific enclosures. Most are designed for easy-installation and to blend with the vehicle's interior for a factory look. But the sound will be anything but factory!

Building a sealed enclosure

01 Using 3/4-inch Medium Density Fiberboard (MDF) for the enclosure, mark the enclosure's measurements and carefully cut the boards

02 Use the template supplied with the subwoofer or the subwoofer mounting ring to mark the positions of the holes, then cut out the holes with a jigsaw

03 When putting the box together, run a bead of glue along the edges of the adjoining seams, then use screws to secure the panels to each other

04 To prevent any air leaks, seal all the seams inside the box with a silicone sealant

05 Using spray glue, cover the box with carpet that'll match your interior, then carefully cut out the holes. You'll also have to drill a hole for the speaker wires

06 Follow the manufacturer's instructions for connecting the subwoofer wiring, then place them into the enclosure and mount them, also according to the manufacturer's instructions

07 Be sure to bolt the sub box down so it doesn't roll around. A loose enclosure can be dangerous, particularly in a crash. The last thing you want during an accident is half a ton of unhappy speaker and box come hurtling in the passenger compartment to remind you they weren't bolted down!

> ⚠ **Warning**
> *Wear a filtering mask before cutting: MDF gives off an extremely fine dust which can be harmful to your health*

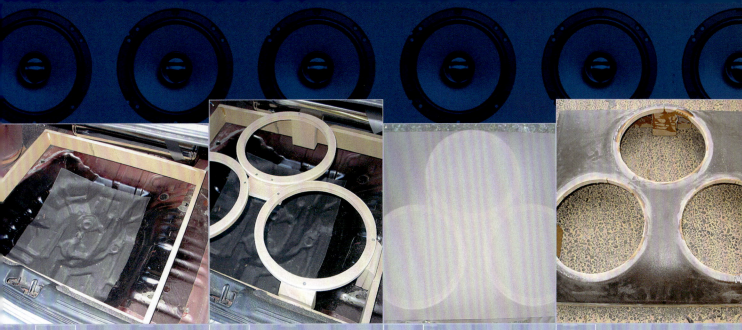

01	The trunk area was stripped of the spare tire to make room for the enclosure, and a support frame was constructed of 3/4-inch Medium Density Fiberboard (MDF)
02	We fabricated rings to hold the subwoofers. The rings are tied in the center by a piece of MDF glued to the bottom, then secured by screws through the top
03	We stretched speaker fabric over the top of the box, secured it with staples, then cut out the holes. Then we brushed a coat of fiberglass resin on both sides
04	After the resin completely dried . . .

Building a custom fiberglass enclosure

Warning: Wear a filtering mask before cutting: MDF gives off an extremely fine dust which can be harmful to your health

05	. . . we reinforced the inside of the box with steel mesh and body filler
06	We also applied a coat of body filler to the exterior to fill in any imperfections . . .
07	. . . then sanded, primered and sanded again for a smooth surface that's ready for the paint shop
08	After returning from the paint shop the box is placed in its final resting spot, then the subs are wired up and mounted

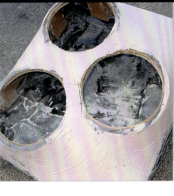

Video

Watch TV... pop in a movie on DVD... play a video game... mobile video now lets you do it all.

The simplest mobile video systems are portable, self-contained units which can be strapped into place between the two front seats. There are other systems similar to these, but they are built into the center console and aren't easily removed like the portable type.

The other kind of system is the component type. All component systems begin at the source unit, which could take the form of a remotely mounted VHS tape deck or DVD player, in-dash DVD player, an overhead flip-down screen with an integral DVD player, a Sony PlayStation, a TV tuner or a combination of these. This source signal is then directed to one or more monitors. Some in-dash DVD players have an integral motorized screen that retracts when not in use. When multiple source units are used, they must be connected to a signal distribution box (switcher) installed between the source units and the monitor(s).

Monitor types include the already-mentioned in-dash motorized screen, sunshade monitors, headrest monitors, flip-down overhead console monitors, center console monitors, and monitors that can be mounted on a pedestal or bracket just about anywhere in the vehicle that there's enough room. Just keep in mind that no screen visible to the driver can be operational when the vehicle is in motion.

Video game consoles can be integrated into the system by the use of a signal distribution box and a power inverter that converts 12 volts DC into 110 volts AC. And, with the use of the proper switchbox, a video game can be played on one monitor while a movie is watched on another.

Another neat option that's available with some systems are infrared headphones that allow passengers to listen to the movie or game audio track without the hassle of cords that could get in the way. The infrared signal on these systems is broadcast from transmitters embedded in the monitor housings or from a remote transmitter, usually mounted on the headliner or at the rear of the overhead console where the line-of-sight between the transmitter and headphone will be uninterrupted.

Audio can also be piped through the vehicle's existing speakers. If you've upgraded your audio system with a surround sound system, your passengers will be able to enjoy a near-theatre experience. Just don't let them spill their drinks on the floor, throw bon-bons at the screen or stick their chewing gum to the underside of the seats!

Security

Avoiding trouble

Those shiny wheels and flashy paint are like a billboard to car thieves and bandits looking for expensive sound system components to sell on the black market. And you've got to be careful when and where you choose to show off your car's mobile entertainment, and to whom. Be especially discreet the nearer you get to home - turn your system down before you get near home, for instance, or you might draw unwelcome attention to where that car with the loud stereo's parked at night.

If you're going out, think about where you're parking - somewhere well-lit and reasonably well-populated is the best bet.

If you're lucky enough to have a garage, use it. And always use all the security you have, whenever you leave the car, even if it's a tedious chore to put on that steering wheel lock. Just do it.

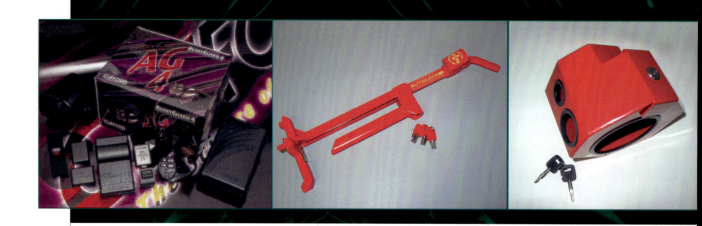

Alarms

Alarm systems are available in many different packages depending on cost and complexity. Here are just a few examples of types of alarm system sensors designed for different types of protection.

A more sophisticated alarm will feature shock sensing (which could be set off by a thief attempting to steal your tires); this type of sensor monitors the impact/vibration level.

Ultrasonic sensors monitor an enclosed space inside of a vehicle (such as the passenger compartment) with

Anti-theft devices

Other types of anti-theft devices are available as less expensive alternative to alarms.

An automobile equipped with a steering wheel lock or a removable steering wheel could make your car a less likely target for a thief. Also available are locking covers for the steering column which can help prevent a thief from being able to access the ignition lock, and devices that prevent the brake or clutch pedal from being depressed. Whatever your choice may be, now every time you park, at least you can relax a little. Remember, though, there's no guarantee that installing an alarm or security device will make any difference to a determined thief or mindless vandal.

If your vehicle is equipped with an alarm system or an anti-theft device, you may be eligible for discounted insurance premiums. Certain companies offer a higher percentage discount for vehicles that have more sophisticated alarm system packages. Each insurance company will have their own guidelines and insurance discounts. Contact your insurance representative for all the specific details.

Wiring basics

Security

ultrasonic sound waves. If the sensor detects a change in the sound waves the alarm will sound.

Field Disturbance Sensors protect an area with an energy shield. Similar to ultrasonic sensors, FDS sensors monitor the space inside of a vehicle. They are often used to protect the passenger compartment of a convertible with the top down.

Pin switches typically monitor the doors, hoods or trunks by completing the circuit and activating the alarm when one of these has been opened.

Many suppliers have designed security systems not only to protect a vehicle; some are designed to give added convenience with packages that allow you to add onto the alarm network, such as keyless entry, power window control or remote starting capability. When purchasing an alarm, be sure to take the time and study each kit and their advantages and shortcomings.

With your wires identified, how to tap into them? The three best options are:

a **Soldering** - *avoids cutting through your chosen wire - strip away a short section of insulation, wrap your new wire around the bared section, then apply solder to secure it. If you're a bit new to soldering, practice on a few spare pieces of wire first.*

b **Bullet connectors** - *cut and strip the end of your chosen wire, wrap your new one to it, push both into one half of the bullet. Connect the other end of your victim wire to the other bullet, and connect together. Always use the "female" half on any live feed - it'll be safer if you disconnect it than a male bullet, which could touch bare metal and send your car up in smoke.*

c **Block connectors** - *easy to use. Just remember that the wires can come adrift if the screws aren't really tight, and don't get too ambitious about how many wires you can stuff in one hole (block connectors, like bullets, are available in several sizes).*

With any of these options, always insulate around your connection - especially when soldering, or you'll be leaving bare metal exposed. Remember that you'll probably be shoving all the wires up into the dark recesses of the under-dash area - by the time the wires are nice and kinked/squashed together, that tiny bit of protruding wire might just touch that bit of metal bodywork.

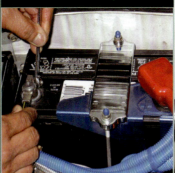
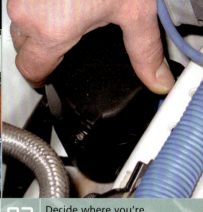

01 Disconnect the cable from the negative battery terminal, and move the cable away from the battery. This will probably wipe out your stereo settings, but it's better than having sparks flying and your new alarm chirping during installation

02 Decide where you're going to mount the siren. Choose somewhere not easily reached from underneath. Try the siren in position before deciding. It's also best to pick a location away from where you'll be adding fluids to the window washer reservoir, oil to the engine or coolant to the radiator. Loosely fit the alarm to the bracket, to help you decide how well it'll fit in your chosen spot, then take the alarm away

Alarm installation

Installing an alarm system can be one of the best investments you make in your car. Most alarms are fairly easy to install. We'll run through a typical installation here, but you should follow the specific instructions that will come with the alarm you chose.

Warning:
Whenever working on a vehicle equipped with an airbag (or airbags), be sure to disable the airbag system before working in the vicinity of any airbag system components. This is especially important when working around the instrument panel and center console. Consult the Haynes Automotive Repair Manual for your vehicle for the airbag disabling procedure. If no manual exists, consult a dealer service department or other qualified repair shop to obtain the information. Also, NEVER splice or tap into any wiring for the airbag system, and never use a test light or multimeter on airbag system wiring. On most vehicles the wiring for the airbag system is yellow, or is covered by yellow conduit, or at the very least will have yellow electrical connectors.

Mark the position of the mounting holes, then carefully drill the holes (make sure there's nothing behind the panel you're drilling). Once you've got the bracket where you want it, install and tighten the mounting bracket screws **03**

04 The next stage is to sort your wiring. The amount of wiring, and where you'll want to run it, will depend on your alarm. If, like us, you've got wires coming from the siren which should be fed into the car, you'll need to feed them through somehow. We chose a cover on the firewall, which we removed, then drilled a hole big enough for the wires to pass through

05 Clean up any rough edges from the hole, then insert a grommet. If you don't, there's a good chance the wires will chafe through on the metal edges

06 If you've got several wires to go through, as we did, tape them together into a makeshift "loom", which will make it much easier to poke the wires through

07 After moving inside the car, with the help of an assistant, the alarm wiring was soon poked through. It's worth sealing any holes you make in the firewall (with silicone), to reduce the chance of water getting in. Make sure any wires running into the engine bay from the firewall run down and not up - this will minimize chances of water getting into your passenger compartment

08 Slip in the siren and tighten the bolts

09 All alarms worth having will have an LED to indicate the alarm status, and to hopefully deter thieves. The easiest option for mounting an LED is to pick one of the blank switches (if your vehicle is equipped with one), pry it out of the dash . . .

10 . . . and drill it for the LED holder

The best way to connect to any existing wiring without cutting it is to solder on your new alarm wires. It's permanent, won't come loose, and doesn't mess up the original circuit. Strip a little insulation off your target wire and the end of the alarm wire. Twist one around the other, if possible **15**

16 Now bring in the soldering iron, heat the connection, and join the wires together with solder (be careful not to burn yourself, the dash, or the surrounding wires!)

17 Remember - whatever method you use for joining the new wires (and especially if you're soldering) - insulate the new connection big-time. The last thing you want is false alarms, other electrical problems, or even a fire, caused by poorly-insulated connections.

18 Many alarms require you to link into the turn signal circuit, so the lights flash during arming and disarming. On our vehicle, the turn signal circuit could be accessed at the fuse panel. After temporarily reconnecting the battery and switching on the indicators, we test with our meter, and find this to be true

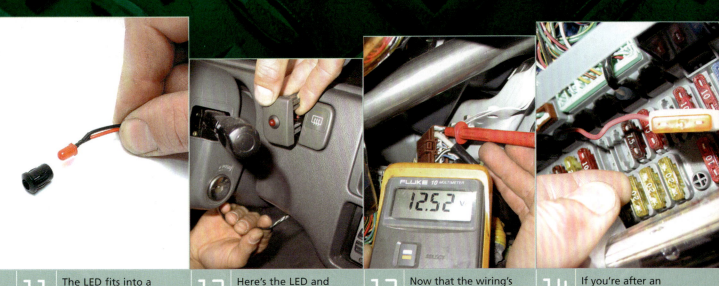

11 The LED fits into a holder, which then fits into the hole. Assemble the LED and holder before installing

12 Here's the LED and holder being installed

13 Now that the wiring's more or less in the right place, it's time to start connecting it up. Power and grounds can be sourced from the fuse panel. When you've found a likely suspect, use a 12-volt test light (available at just about any auto parts store) or voltmeter to confirm your suspicions. We found power at the back of a connector for the steering column

14 If you're after an ignition power circuit, probe the wire with the voltmeter or test light tip (or push it carefully into the back of the wiring connector) and attach the clip to a good ground (like one of the door pin switch screws) - check that it's a switched circuit by temporarily reconnecting the battery and turning the ignition on and off, which should turn power on and off. It's best to tap into the fused side of any wire - to check for this, pull the fuse from the fuse panel, and make sure your chosen wire goes dead

19 The control unit requires its own ground. Find a spot to mount it to the vehicle chassis. Be sure to sand off any paint so that the connection is made directly to metal

20 Next on our wire target list - the power locks. With luck, finding the doors "lock" and "unlock" trigger wires shouldn't be difficult. The most likely place to find them is in the driver's door harness. More stripping and soldering had these wires joined to the relevant ones

21 So come on - does it work? Most alarms require you to "program in" the remotes before they'll work. Test all the alarm features in turn, remembering to follow the alarm's instructions. Set the anti-shock sensitivity with a thought to where you live and park - will it be set off every night by the neighbor's cat, or by kids playing football? Finally, and most important of all - next time you park, remember to set it!

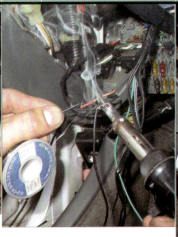

10-5

Security

Remote Power locks

If your ride doesn't have power locks, don't despair - there's several kits out there to help you towards your goal. Hopefully, the details below, together with your kit's instructions, will help you out.

01 First, remove the door trim panel. Most door panels are secured by a few screws, and push-in plastic fasteners around the perimeter of the panel (if necessary refer to the Haynes Automotive Repair Manual for your vehicle). Carefully peel back the plastic sheet from the door, ideally without ripping it

06 . . . then, it's going to get a trim

07 Connect the rods with the supplied clamp . . .

08 . . . then fasten the clamp screws tight

02 The new lock solenoids must be mounted so they work in the same plane as the door lock buttons. What this means is it's no good having the lock solenoid plungers moving vertically, to work a button and rod which operate horizontally! Try it in place, and see where it can be mounted. Looks like we need to drill holes for this one . . .

03 . . . then, once the holes are drilled, screws mount it to the door

04 The kit contains several items which look like bike spokes - these are your new lock operating rods, which join the door lock button operating rod to the lock solenoid

05 This mounting location is going to require the solenoid rod to be bent a little . . .

09 That's the mechanical side done, all that's left to do now is the wiring

10 You've got to feed the solenoid wires through the door and into the car . . .

11 . . . normally there's a handy rubber boot at the door edge you can pry out and feed the wires through into the passenger compartment

12 Once you've managed that, you can connect the wires to your alarm system's control unit "trigger inputs" and give it a try

Safety First

Regardless of how enthusiastic you may be about getting on with the job at hand, take the time to ensure that your safety is not jeopardized. A moment's lack of attention can result in an accident, as can failure to observe certain simple safety precautions. The possibility of an accident will always exist, and the following points should not be considered a comprehensive list of all dangers. Rather, they are intended to make you aware of the risks and to encourage a safety conscious approach to all work you carry out on your vehicle.

Essential DOs and DON'Ts

DON'T rely on a jack when working under the vehicle. Always use approved jackstands to support the weight of the vehicle and place them under the recommended lift or support points.

DON'T attempt to loosen extremely tight fasteners (i.e. wheel lug nuts) while the vehicle is on a jack - it may fall.

DON'T start the engine without first making sure that the transmission is in Neutral (or Park where applicable) and the parking brake is set.

DON'T remove the cooling system pressure cap from a hot cooling system - let it cool or cover it with a cloth and release the pressure gradually.

DON'T attempt to drain the engine oil until you are sure it has cooled to the point that it will not burn you.

DON'T touch any part of the engine or exhaust system until it has cooled sufficiently to avoid burns.

DON'T siphon toxic liquids such as gasoline, antifreeze and brake fluid by mouth, or allow them to remain on your skin.

DON'T inhale brake lining dust - it is potentially hazardous (see **Asbestos**).

DON'T allow spilled oil or grease to remain on the floor - wipe it up before someone slips on it.

DON'T use loose fitting wrenches or other tools which may slip and cause injury.

DON'T push on wrenches when loosening or tightening nuts or bolts. Always try to pull the wrench toward you. If the situation calls for pushing the wrench away, push with an open hand to avoid scraped knuckles if the wrench should slip.

DON'T attempt to lift a heavy component alone - get someone to help you.

DON'T rush or take unsafe shortcuts to finish a job.

DON'T allow children or animals in or around the vehicle while you are working on it.

DO wear eye protection when using power tools such as a drill, sander, bench grinder, etc. and when working under a vehicle.

DO keep loose clothing and long hair well out of the way of moving parts.

DO make sure that any hoist used has a safe working load rating adequate for the job.

DO get someone to check on you periodically when working alone on a vehicle.

DO carry out work in a logical sequence and make sure that everything is correctly assembled and tightened.

DO keep chemicals and fluids tightly capped and out of the reach of children and pets.

DO remember that your vehicle's safety affects that of yourself and others. If in doubt on any point, get professional advice.

Steering, suspension and brakes

These systems are essential to driving safety, so make sure you have a qualified shop or individual check your work. Also, compressed suspension springs can cause injury if released suddenly - be sure to use a spring compressor.

Airbag

Airbags are explosive devices that can cause injury if they deploy while you're working on the car. Follow the manufacturer's instructions to disable the airbag whenever you're working in the vicinity of airbag components. Never use airbag system wiring when installing electronic components. When in doubt, check your vehicle's wiring diagram.

Asbestos

Certain friction, insulating, sealing, and other products - such as brake linings, brake bands, clutch linings, torque converters, gaskets, etc. - may contain asbestos or other hazardous friction material. Extreme care must be taken to avoid inhalation of dust from such products, since it is hazardous to health. If in doubt, assume that they are harmful.

Fire

Remember at all times that gasoline is highly flammable. Never smoke or have any kind of open flame around when working on a vehicle. But the risk does not end there. A spark caused by an electrical short circuit, by two metal surfaces contacting each other, by a tool falling on concrete, or even by static electricity built up in your body under certain conditions, can ignite gasoline vapors, which in a confined space are highly explosive. Do not, under any circumstances, use gasoline for cleaning parts. Use an approved safety solvent.

Always disconnect the battery ground (-) cable at the battery before working on any part of the fuel system or electrical system. Never risk spilling fuel on a hot engine or exhaust component. It is strongly recommended that a fire extinguisher suitable for use on fuel and electrical fires be kept handy in the garage or workshop at all times. Never try to extinguish a fuel or electrical fire with water.

Fumes

Certain fumes are highly toxic and can quickly cause unconsciousness and even death if inhaled to any extent. Gasoline vapor falls into this category, as do the vapors from some cleaning solvents. Any draining or pouring of such volatile fluids should be done in a well ventilated area.

When using cleaning fluids and solvents, read the instructions on the container carefully. Never use materials from unmarked containers.

Never run the engine in an enclosed space, such as a garage. Exhaust fumes contain carbon monoxide, which is extremely poisonous. If you need to run the engine, always do so in the open air, or at least have the rear of the vehicle outside the work area.

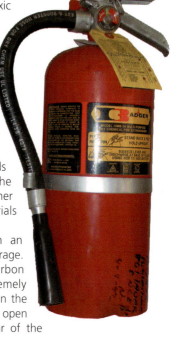

The battery

Never create a spark or allow a bare light bulb near a battery. They normally give off a certain amount of hydrogen gas, which is highly explosive.

Always disconnect the battery ground (-) cable at the battery before working on the fuel or electrical systems.

If possible, loosen the filler caps or cover when charging the battery from an external source (this does not apply to sealed or maintenance-free batteries). Do not charge at an excessive rate or the battery may burst.

Take care when adding water to a non maintenance-free battery and when carrying a battery. The electrolyte, even when diluted, is very corrosive and should not be allowed to contact clothing or skin.

Always wear eye protection when cleaning the battery to prevent the caustic deposits from entering your eyes.

Household current

When using an electric power tool, inspection light, etc., which operates on household current, always make sure that the tool is correctly connected to its plug and that, where necessary, it is properly grounded. Do not use such items in damp conditions and, again, do not create a spark or apply excessive heat in the vicinity of fuel or fuel vapor.

Secondary ignition system voltage

A severe electric shock can result from touching certain parts of the ignition system (such as the spark plug wires) when the engine is running or being cranked, particularly if components are damp or the insulation is defective. In the case of an electronic ignition system, the secondary system voltage is much higher and could prove fatal.

Glossary of terms

A

Acceleration - The time rate of change in velocity; velocity (speed) can be measured in feet-per-second, acceleration in feet-per-second-per-second, or feet-per-second-squared.

Adhesion - The property of oil which causes it to cling to metal surfaces such as bearings. Also, the ability of a tire to remain in contact with a road surface. Also, the ability of a paint to stick to the surface being painted.

Advance - Moving the timing of the camshaft, distributor spark or valve operation ahead so that an event - such as firing of the spark plug or the opening of a valve - occurs earlier in the cycle. This term is also used to describe the mechanism used for accomplishing this.

Air-fuel mixture - The air and fuel traveling to the combustion chamber after being mixed by the carburetor, or after fuel is injected into the airstream by an injector. The mass of air supplied to the engine, divided by the mass of fuel supplied in the same period of time. The *stoichiometric*, or chemically correct, air-fuel ratio (*AFR*, or *A/F ratio*) is the exact ratio necessary to burn all the carbon and hydrogen in the fuel, leaving no other combustion by-products except carbon dioxide and water. See *stoichiometric*.

Air-fuel ratio - The ratio of air to the *weight* of the fuel supplied to the mixture for combustion. See *stoichiometric*.

Air gap - Space between spark plug electrodes, starting motor and generator armatures, field shoes, etc.

Air pressure - Atmospheric pressure (14.7 psi).

Air-to-air intercooler - A heat exchanger, used on a turbocharged engine, which uses ambient air to cool the air coming from the turbo into the intake manifold.

Air-to-water intercooler - A heat exchanger, used on a turbocharged engine, which uses liquid coolant from the radiator to cool the air coming from the turbo into the intake manifold.

Alloy - A metal containing two or more elements. Adding one or more elements to a pure metal alters its properties such as elongation, strength, etc. For example: solder is an alloy of lead and tin.

Alloy wheel - A generic term used to describe any non-steel road wheel. The alloys are usually aluminum of magnesium (hence the term *mag wheel*, which refers to any non-steel wheel).

All-wheel-drive (AWD) - A vehicle drivetrain with every wheel under power. On a four-wheeled vehicle, all-wheel-drive generally refers to a full-time four-wheel-drive system with a center differential.

Anti-seize compound - A coating that reduces the risk of seizing on fasteners that are subjected to high temperatures, such as exhaust manifold bolts and nuts.

Aspect ratio - The ratio of section height to section width on a tire.

ATDC - "After Top Dead Center," the point at which a piston starts to move downward in the cylinder on either the intake stroke or the combustion stroke.

B

Backpressure - Any resistance to free flow in the exhaust system. For example, catalytic converters and mufflers cause backpressure.

Ball bearing - An anti-friction bearing consisting of a hardened inner and outer race with hardened steel balls interposed between two races.

Balance shaft(s) - The rotating shaft or shafts, incorporating eccentric counterweights, designed to counter-act the natural vibration of other reciprocating parts, such as the pistons, connecting rods and crankshaft.

Balancing - The process of checking every engine part for conformity to its specified dimensions. The specified working clearances for all moving parts are also checked. Balancing improves engine performance, smoothness and reliability. Also referred to as *blueprinting*.

Banjo fitting - A type of hydraulic fitting, shaped like a banjo, through which a hollow bolt passes, allowing fluid transfer from a hydraulic line to a hydraulic component.

Barometric pressure (or Bar) - Atmospheric pressure, expressed in inches of Mercury (in-Hg). Barometric pressure is determined by how high atmospheric pressure (relative to zero absolute pressure) forces Mercury up a glass tube. 14.5 psi = 29.92 inches.

BDC - "Bottom Dead Center." The lowest point of piston and connecting rod travel in the cylinder; the ends of the intake and power strokes, respectively, in a four-stroke engine.

Black smoke - Incompletely burned fuel in the exhaust.

Block deck - The cylinder head gasket surface.

Blow-by - The leakage of the compressed air-fuel mixture or the burned gases from the combustion chamber past the piston rings and into the crankcase. this leakage results in power loss and oil contamination.

Blower - A pump-like device which forces air into the cylinders at higher-than-atmospheric pressure. Because of this higher pressure, the cylinder gets more air per intake stroke, which means it can burn more fuel, which means more horsepower. There are two types of blowers - A turbocharger uses some of the waste heat energy in the exhaust gases to drive a compressor and pump the air; a belt-driven supercharger uses engine power to pump air. See *turbocharger* and *supercharger*. The term also refers to the *blower motor fan* assembly in the heating/air conditioning system.

Blow-off valve - A control valve on a turbocharged engine, installed on the intake side of the system, which relieves pressure if it exceeds a predetermined value.

Blueprinting - Dismantling an engine and reassembling it to EXACT specifications.

Blue smoke - Caused by blow-by allowing crankcase oil in the combustion chamber due to bad rings, valve seals or other faulty components.

Bore diameter - Diameter of the cylinders.

Bottom end - A term which refers collectively to the engine block, crankshaft, main bearings and the big ends of the connecting rods.

Brake horsepower (bhp) - The power produced by the engine (as measured at the output shaft) that is available for driving the vehicle. It's called brake horsepower because the shaft power is usually measured by an absorption dynamometer or *brake*.

Break-in - The period of operation between installation of new or rebuilt parts and the point in time at which the parts are worn to the correct fit. The time or mileage period during which the rough edges and friction between newly assembled moving parts and surfaces are gradually reduced. Generally calls for moderate loads and driving at reduced and varying speed for a specified mileage to permit parts to wear to the correct fit.

BTDC - "Before Top Dead Center;" any position of the piston between bottom dead center and top dead center, on the upward stroke.

C

Cam - A rotating lobe or eccentric which, when used with a cam follower, can change rotary motion to the reciprocating motion. For example, the multi-lobed *breaker cam* rotating in the inanition distributor interrupts the primary circuit to induce a high tension spark for ignition. Some brake adjuster designs use a cam (or cams) to set the clearance between the brake shoes and brake drum.

Cam follower - A device that follows the cam contour as it rotates. Also called a lifter, valve lifter or tappet.

Camshaft - A rotating shaft on which a series of *cam lobes* operate the valve mechanisms. The camshaft is driven by gears or sprockets and a timing chain. Usually referred to simply as the *cam*.

Camshaft gear - The sprocket used to drive the camshaft.

Case harden - To harden the surface of steel.

Cast iron - An alloy of iron and more than two percent carbon, used for engine blocks and heads because it's relatively inexpensive and easy to mold into complex shapes.

Catalytic converter - A muffler-like device in the exhaust system that catalyzes a chemical reaction which converts certain air pollutants in the exhaust gases into less harmful substances.

Cavitation - A condition in which a partial vacuum forms around the blades or impeller wheels of a pump, reducing the pump's output because part of the pump blades lose contact with the liquid. It can be a problem in fuel and water pumps, fluid couplings and torque converters and, when severe, can result in erosion of pump blades and other internal surfaces.

Central Fuel Injection (CFI) - A computer-controlled fuel metering system which sprays atomized fuel into a throttle body mounted on the intake manifold.

Chamfer - To bevel across - or, a bevel on - the sharp edge of an object or a hole.

Closed loop - An operating condition or mode which enables modification of programmed instructions based on a feedback system.

Closed loop fuel control - The normal operating mode for a fuel injection system. Once the engine is warmed up the computer can interpret an analog voltage signal from an exhaust gas oxygen sensor and alter the air/fuel ratio accordingly through the fuel injectors.

Closed loop mode - Once the engine has reached "warm-up" temperature, the engine management computer collects the precise data from all the sensors (coolant temperature sensor, throttle position sensor, oxygen sensor etc.) to determine the most efficient air/fuel mixture for combustion.

Clutch - Any device which connects and disconnects a driven component from the driving component. For example a clutch is used to disengage the engine from the transmission in vehicles with a manual transmission.

Coil binding - Compressing a valve spring to the point at which each coil touches the adjacent coil.

Cold lash - The valve lash clearance, measured between the rocker arm and valve tip, when the engine is cold.

Collapsed piston - A piston whose skirt diameter has been reduced by heat and the forces imposed upon it during service in engine.

Combustion chamber - The cavity in the cylinder head (or the cylinder head and the piston) into which the air/fuel mixture is compressed by the piston when the piston is at the top of its compression stroke. In other words, the volume of the cylinder above the piston with the piston at top dead center.

Compression - Reduction in volume, and increase in pressure and temperature, of a gas, caused by squeezing it into a smaller space.

Compression ratio - The relationship between cylinder volume (clearance volume) when the piston is at top dead center and cylinder volume when the piston is at bottom dead center. The clearance volume of an engine cylinder divided by its total volume.

Compression ring - The upper ring, or rings, on a piston, designed to hold the compression in the combustion chamber and prevent blow-by.

Compression stroke - The piston's movement from bottom dead center to top dead center immediately following the intake stroke, during which both the intake and exhaust valves are closed while the air-fuel mixture in the cylinder is compressed.

Compressor - The part of a turbocharger that compresses the intake air.

Compressor pressure ratio - In a turbocharger system, the ratio between the absolute pressure at the compressor outlet and the absolute pressure at the compressor inlet.

Compressor ratio - In a turbocharged engine, the ratio between the volume in the cylinder when the piston is at the bottom of its stroke and the volume in the cylinder when the piston is at the top of its stroke.

Computer - A device that takes information, processes it, makes decisions and outputs those decisions.

Connecting rod - The rod that connects the crank on the crankshaft with the piston. Sometimes called a con rod.

Connecting rod cap - The part of the connecting rod assembly that attaches the rod to the crankpin.

Constant velocity (CV) joint - A universal joint whose output shaft travels at the same velocity as the input shaft, through 360-degrees, with no fluctuations in speed.

Coolant temperature sensor - A device that senses the engine coolant temperature, and passes that information to the electronic control module as an analog (variable) voltage signal.

Core plug - Soft metal plug used to plug the casting holes for the coolant passages in the block. See *freeze plug*.

Counterbalancing - Additional weight placed at the crankshaft vibration damper an/or flywheel to balance the crankshaft.

Counterbore - Concentric machine surface around a hole opening. To enlarge a hole to a given depth.

Crankcase - The lower part of the engine in which the crankshaft rotates; includes the lower section of the cylinder block and the oil pan.

Crankcase breather - A port or tube that vents fumes from the crankcase. An inlet breather allows fresh air into the crankcase.

Crankcase dilution - Under certain conditions of operation, unburned portions of fuel get past piston rings into the crankcase where they "thin" the engine lubricating oil.

Crank kit - A reground or reconditioned crankshaft and new main and connecting rod bearings.

Crankpin - The part of a crankshaft to which a connecting rod is attached.

Crankshaft - The main rotating member, or shaft, running the length of the crankcase, with offset throws to which the connecting rods are attached; changes the reciprocating motion of the pistons into rotating motion.

Crankshaft counterbalance - Series of weights attached to, or forged integrally, with the crankshaft and placed to offset reciprocating weight of each piston and rod assembly.

Crankshaft gear - The gear on the front of the crankshaft which drives the camshaft gear.

Cylinder block - Largest single part of an engine. Basic or main mass of metal in which cylinders are bored or placed.

Cylinder head - A detachable portion of an engine fastened securely to cylinder block which contains all or a portion of combustion chamber.

Cylinder head gasket - Seal between engine block and cylinder head.

Cylinder sleeve - A replaceable sleeve, or liner, pressed into the cylinder block to form the cylinder bore and provide a replaceable friction surface for the piston and rings.

D

Deck - The flat upper surface of the engine block where the cylinder head mounts.

Deck height - The center of the crankshaft main-bearing bores to the block deck surface.

Degree wheel - A disc divided into 360 equal parts that can be attached to a shaft to measure angle of rotation.

Density - The weight or mass per unit volume of a gas, liquid or solid. Density is an indicator of relative compactness of a mass of matter in a given volume.

Detonation - The uncontrolled spontaneous explosion of air/fuel mixture in the combustion chamber - after the spark occurs at the spark plug - which spontaneously combusts the remaining air/fuel mixture, resulting in a "pinging" noise, and causing a loss of power and possible engine damage. Commonly referred to as spark knock or ping.

Detonation-activated ignition retard - A system which retards the ignition timing when the detonation knock sensor picks up vibration at frequencies typical of detonation.

Detonation sensor - A device, usually piezoelectric, which senses frequencies typical of detonation and converts this information into an analog voltage signal. Also called a *knock sensor*.

Dial indicator - A precision measuring instrument that indicates movement to a thousandth of an inch with a needle sweeping around dial face.

Dish - A depression in the top of a piston.

Displacement - The total volume of an engine's cylinders, usually measured in cubic inches, cubic centimeters or liters. The total volume of air-fuel mixture an engine is theoretically capable of drawing into all cylinders during one operating cycle. Also refers to the volume swept out by the piston as it moves from bottom dead center to top dead center.

Distributor - In the ignition system on a spark-ignition engine, a mechanical device designed to switch a high voltage secondary circuit from an ignition coil to the spark plugs in the proper firing sequence.

Double-overhead cam (DOHC) - An engine that uses two overhead camshafts, one for the intake valves and one for the exhaust valves. The cams are driven by a timing chain or by a timing belt.

Draw-through - A turbocharger system in which the turbocharger sucks the air/fuel mixture through the carburetor or fuel injector, i.e. the air and fuel mixing occurs upstream from the turbocharger.

Drivebelt(s) - The belt(s) used to drive accessories such as the alternator, water pump, power steering pump, air conditioning compressor, etc. off the crankshaft pulley.

Drivetrain - The power-transmitting components in a vehicle. Usually consists of the clutch (on vehicles with a manual transmission), the (manual or automatic) transmission, the driveshaft, the universal joints, the differential and the driveaxle assemblies.

Dry sump - A lubrication system in which the engine's supply of oil isn't contained in the crankcase (sump), but is pumped to the engine from an external container. Allows the crankcase to be reduced in size and the engine to be reduced in size and the engine to be installed lower in the chassis, and eliminates the oil starvation most conventional oiling systems suffer when subjected to the acceleration, braking and cornering forces generated by a racing vehicle.

Duration - The period of time during which anything lasts. For a camshaft, the time each valve is open, measured in crankshaft degrees of rotation.

Duty cycle - Many solenoid-operated metering devices cycle on and off. The duty cycle is a measurement of the amount of time a device is energized, or turned on, expressed as a percentage of the complete on-off cycle of that

device. In other words, the duty cycle is the ratio of the pulse width to the complete cycle width.
Dynamometer - A device for measuring the power output, or brake horsepower, of an engine. An engine dynamometer measures the power output at the flywheel. A chassis dynamometer measures power at the drive wheels.

E

Eccentric - One circle within another circle not having the same center. A disk, or offset section (of a shaft, for example) used to convert rotary motion to reciprocating motion. Sometimes called a cam.
EGR valve - A valve used to introduce exhaust gases into the intake air stream to lower exhaust emissions, principally oxides of nitrogen (NOx).
Electronically-controlled wastegate - A turbocharger wastegate that's activated by an electric signal from a computer.
Electronic Control Module (ECM) - A generic term referring to the computer. The ECM is the brain of the engine control systems receiving information from various sensors in the engine compartment. The ECM calculates what is required for proper engine operation and controls the different actuators to achieve it.
Electronic Fuel Injection (EFI) - A computer-controlled fuel system that distributes fuel through an injector located in each intake port of the engine.
Electronic ignition - An ignition system that uses electronic switching devices to relieve the mechanical breaker points of part of their duties or replace them. Electronic ignitions can be divided into three basic classifications - contact controlled, mechanically controlled and capacitor controlled. In the first type, the breaker points are retained but merely serve to trigger a transistor which switches the heavy primary current. In a magnetically controlled (also known as a *contactless* or *all-electronic*) system, transistors are used as the switching device for the primary current and the points are eliminated. A capacitive discharge system can be either all-electronic or breaker-point controlled (although points haven't been used since the Seventies).
Engine block - The iron or aluminum casting which encloses the crankshaft, connecting rods, connecting rods and pistons.
Engine displacement - The sum of piston displacement of all engine cylinders.
Exhaust manifold – Attached to the cylinder head, the exhaust manifold collects the exhaust from all engine exhaust ports and routes the exhaust gasses into a single exhaust pipe. Exhaust manifolds are usually made from cast iron, which contains heat and noise well and has excellent durability at high temperatures. A common performance modification is to replace the exhaust manifold with a tubular-steel header, which often offers better performance, but usually is not as durable and increases underhood heat and noise.
Exhaust oxygen sensor - Also known as an *oxygen sensor* or an *02 sensor*. Device that detects the amount of oxygen in the exhaust stream, and sends that information to the ECM.
Exhaust ports - The passages in the cylinder head, connecting the exhaust valves and the exhaust manifold, through which the exhaust gases pass on their way to the exhaust manifold.
Exhaust stroke - The portion of the piston's movement devoted to expelling burned gases from the cylinder. The exhaust stroke lasts from bottom dead center to top dead center, immediately following the power stroke, during which the exhaust valve opens so the exhaust gases can escape from the cylinder to the exhaust manifold.
Exhaust system - The pipes, resonators and mufflers that carry the exhaust gases from the exhaust manifold out into the atmosphere.
Exhaust valve - The valve through which the burned air-fuel charge passes on its way from the cylinder to the exhaust manifold during the exhaust stroke.

F

Feeler gauge - A thin strip or blade of hardened steel, ground to an exact thickness, used to check and/or measure clearances between parts. Feeler gauges are graduated in thickness by increments of .001 inch.
Firing order - The order in which the engine cylinders fire, or deliver their power strokes, beginning with the number one cylinder.
Flare-nut wrench - A wrench designed for loosening hydraulic fitting tube nuts (flare-nuts) without damaging them. Flare-nut wrenches are kind of like a six-point box-end wrench with one of the flats missing, which allows the wrench to pass over the tubing but still maintain a maximum amount of contact with the nut.
Float - Float occurs when the valve train loses contact with the cam lobe and the parts "float" on air until control is regained.
Flywheel - A heavy, usually metal, spinning wheel in which energy is absorbed and stored by means of momentum. On cars, the heavy metal wheel that's attached to the crankshaft to smooth out firing impulses. It provides inertia to keep the crankshaft turning smoothly during periods when no power is being applied. It also serves as part of the clutch and engine cranking systems.
Foot-pound - A unit of measurement for work, equal to lifting one pound one foot.
Four-stroke cycle - The four piston strokes - intake, compression, power and exhaust - that make up the complete cycle of events in the four-stroke cycle engine. Also referred to as four-cycle and four-stroke.
Freeze plug - A disc or cup-shaped metal device inserted in a hole in a casting through which core was removed when casting was formed. Also known as a *core hole plug* or *expansion plug*. See *core plug*.
Friction horsepower - The amount of power consumed by an engine in driving itself. It includes the power absorbed in mechanical friction and in driving auxiliaries plus, in the case of four-stroke engines, some pumping power.
Fuel injection - A type of fuel system using a pump and injectors instead of a carburetor to meter fuel. There are two main types of injection - continuous, or mechanical (such as Bosch Continuous Injection Systems), and electronic. Mechanical injection systems are no longer manufactured but a wide variety of electronic injection systems can be found on new vehicles. Earlier versions of electronic injection were throttle body designs; these systems utilize one or two injectors in a throttle body above the intake manifold. The latest electronic systems are port injection designs; these systems use one injector at each intake port.
Fuel injector - In electronic fuel-injection systems, a spring-loaded, solenoid (electromagnetic) valve which delivers fuel into the intake manifold, in response to electrical signals from the control module.
Fuel pressure regulator - A pressure-activated diaphragm valve that maintains the pressure in a fuel system to a pre-set value above manifold pressure, particularly in a fuel injection system.
Fuel rail - A special manifold designed to provide a large reservoir of pressurized fuel for the fuel injectors, which are attached between the rail and the intake runners or the cylinder head. The fuel rail also serves as a mounting place for the fuel damper (if equipped) and the fuel pressure regulator.

G

Gallery - A large passage in the engine block that forms a reservoir for engine oil pressure.
Gap - Generally refers to the distance the spark must travel in jumping from the center electrode to the side electrode in a spark plug. Also refers to the spacing between the points in a contact breaker assembly in a conventional points-type ignition, or to the distance between the reluctor or rotor and the pickup coil in an electronic ignition.
Gasket - Any thin, soft material - usually cork, cardboard, asbestos or soft metal - installed between two metal surfaces to ensure a good seal between two components such as the block and the cylinder head.
Gear ratio - Number of revolutions made by a driving gear as compared to number of revolutions made by a driven gear of different size. For example, if one gear makes three revolutions while the other gear makes one revolution, the gear ratio is 3 to 1 or (3:1).

H

Header - A high-performance exhaust manifold that replaces the stock exhaust manifold. Designed with smooth flowing lines to prevent back pressure caused by sharp bends, rough castings, etc. See *Exhaust Manifold*.
Heat range - The ability of a spark plug to transfer heat from the combustion chamber to the cylinder head. The speed of this transfer is commonly described by the terms cold plug and hot plug. A hot plug transfers heat slowly, causing the plug to operate at a higher temperature. A cold plug transfers heat at a faster rate, thus operating at a lower temperature. Plugs are available in different heat ranges to accommodate the operating conditions of different engines and driving conditions. A

plug must operate hot enough to prevent fouling, but cold enough to prevent pre-ignition.
High tension - Secondary or induced high voltage electrical current. Circuit includes wiring from ignition distributor cap to coil and to each spark plug.
Horsepower - A measure of mechanical power, or the rate at which work is done. One horsepower is the amount of power required to lift 550 pounds one foot per second. One horsepower equals 33,000 ft-lbs of work per minute. It's the amount of power necessary to raise 33,000 pounds a distance of one foot in one minute.
Hot lash - The valve adjustment on an engine equipped with solid lifters.

I

Ideal air/fuel mixture, or ideal mixture - The air/fuel ratio which provides the best performance while maintaining maximum conversion of exhaust emissions, typically 14.7:1. See *stoichiometric ratio*.
Idle - Rotational speed of an engine with vehicle at rest and accelerator pedal not depressed.
Idle Air Control (IAC) valve - On fuel-injected vehicles, a valve that allows air to bypass the throttle plate(s), increasing idle speed. The valve is operated by an electric solenoid or motor. The vehicle's computer controls the amount of opening to regulate idle speed for varying conditions such as cold starting and air conditioning compressor load.
Ignition system - The system responsible for igniting fuel in the cylinders. Includes the ignition module, the coil, the coil wire, the distributor, the spark plug wires, the plugs, and a voltage source.
Ignition timing - The moment at which the spark plug fires, usually expressed in the number of crankshaft degrees before the piston reaches the top of its stroke.
Intake manifold - A tube or housing with passages through which flows the air-fuel mixture (carbureted vehicles and vehicles with throttle body injection) or air only (port fuel-injected vehicles) to the port openings in the cylinder head.
Intake ports - The passages in the cylinder head connecting the intake valves and the intake manifold through which the air-fuel mixture flows on its way to the cylinders.
Intake stroke - The portion of the piston's movement, between top dead center and bottom dead center, devoted to drawing fuel mixture into engine cylinder. The intake stroke is the stroke immediately following the exhaust stroke, during which the intake valve opens and the cylinder fills with air-fuel mixture from the intake manifold.
Intake valve - The valve through which the air-fuel mixture is admitted to the cylinder.
Intercooler - A radiator used to reduce the temperature of the compressed air or air/fuel mixture before it enters the combustion chamber. Either air-to-water or, more commonly, air-to-air.
Internal combustion engine - An engine that burns its fuel within cylinders and converts the power of this burning directly into mechanical work.

K

Keeper - The split lock that holds the valve spring retainer in position on the valve stem.
Keyway - A slot cut in a shaft, pulley hub, etc. A square key is placed in the slot and engages a similar keyway in the mating piece.
Knock - The sharp, metallic sound produced when two pressure fronts collide in the combustion chamber of an engine, usually because of *detonation*. Also, a general term used to describe various noises occurring in an engine; can be used to describe noises made by loose or worn mechanical parts, such as a bad bearing. Connecting rod or main bearing knocks are created by too much oil clearance or insufficient lubrication. Also referred to as *detonation*, *pinging* and *spark knock*.
Knurl - A roughened surface caused by a sharp wheel that displaces metal outward as its sharp edges push into the metal surface. To indent or roughen a finished surface.

L

Lean - A term used to describe an air/fuel mixture that's got either too much air or too little fuel.
Lift - Maximum distance and intake or exhaust valve head is raised off its seat.
Lifter - The part that rides against the cam to transfer motion to the rest of the valve train.
Limited slip differential (LSD) - A differential that uses cone or disc clutches to lock the two independent axleshafts together, forcing both wheels to transmit their respective drive torque regardless of the available traction. It allows a limited amount of slip between the two axleshafts to accommodate the differential action. This design doubles the number of drive wheels in low-traction situation.
Lubricant - Any substance, usually oil or grease, applied to moving parts to reduce friction between them.

M

Manifold - Any device designed to collect, route and/or distribute air, air/fuel mixture, exhaust gases, fluids, etc. In air conditioning, a device which controls refrigerant flow for system test purposes by means of hand valves which can open or close various passageways connected together inside the manifold. Used in conjunction with manifold gauges and service hoses. See *exhaust manifold* and *intake manifold*.
Manifold Absolute Pressure (MAP) sensor - A pressure-sensitive disk capacitor used to measure air pressure inside the intake manifold. The MAP sensor sends a signal to the computer which uses this information to determine load conditions so it can adjust spark timing and fuel mixture.

N

Net horsepower - Brake horsepower remaining at flywheel of engine after power required by engine accessories (fan, water pump, alternator, etc.).
Normally-aspirated - An engine which draws its air/fuel mixture into its cylinders solely by piston-created vacuum, i.e. not supercharged or turbocharged.

O

Oil control ring - The third piston ring from the top (and the fourth, if four are used) that scrapes off excess oil from the cylinder walls and returns it to the oil pan via vents in the ring and the piston itself. This action prevents oil from getting into the combustion chamber where it could burn and form carbon that could clog valves and piston rings, short out spark plugs and increase exhaust emissions.
Oil gallery - A pipe or drilled passageway in the engine used to carry engine oil from one area to another.
Oil pan - The detachable lower part of the engine, usually made of stamped steel, which encloses the crankcase and acts as an oil reservoir.
Oil pump - An engine-driven pump that delivers oil to all the moving engine parts. Oil pumps are usually driven from the camshaft either by gears or cams and the two common types are the gear and the rotor pump.
Open-loop fuel control - A non-feedback mode of operation which an engine management system resorts to when the engine is started while it's still cold. During this period, the oxygen sensor isn't yet able to supply reliable data to the computer for controlling the air/fuel mixture ratio because the engine isn't yet warmed up. So mixture control is handled by a program stored in computer memory. Open loop is also used when the engine management system is malfunctioning.
Overhead cam (ohc) engine - An engine with the camshaft(s) located on top of the cylinder head(s) instead of in the engine block. This design eliminates pushrods; some designs also dispense with the rocker arms too. The advantage of an ohc engine are quicker and more accurate valve response because of the shorter path between the cam(s) and the valves.
Overlap - The overlap period occurs at the end of the exhaust stroke and the beginning of the next intake stroke. The exhaust valve closes late to give the burned gases as much time as possible to leave the combustion chamber after they have expended most of their useful work; the intake valve opens early to give the fresh mixture enough time to fill the combustion chamber. The overlap is the number of degrees of crankshaft rotation during which the intake and exhaust valves in one cylinder are open at the same time.
Oxygen sensor - A device installed in the engine exhaust manifold, which senses the oxygen content in the exhaust and converts this information into an electric current.

P

Piston pin (or wrist pin) - The cylindrical and usually hollow steel pin that passes through the piston. The piston pin fastens the piston to the upper end of the connecting rod and serves as the journal for the bearing in the small end of the connecting rod.
Piston ring - The split ring fitted to the groove in a piston. The ring contacts the sides of the ring groove and also rubs against the cylinder wall, thus sealing space between piston and wall. There are two types of rings: Compression rings seal the

11-5

compression pressure in the combustion chamber; oil rings scrape excessive oil off the cylinder wall.
Piston slap - A sound made by a piston with excess skirt clearance as the crankshaft goes across top center.
Port injection - A fuel injection system in which the fuel is sprayed by individual injectors into each intake port, upstream of the intake valve.
Ports - Openings in the cylinder block for the valves, the intake and exhaust manifolds and coolant plumbing. In two-cycle engines, openings for inlet and exhaust purposes.
Positive Crankcase Ventilation (PCV) system - An emission control system that routes engine crankcase fumes into the intake manifold or air cleaner, where they are drawn into the cylinders and burned along with the air-fuel mixture.
Powertrain - The components through which motive power is generated and transmitted to the driven axles. See *drivetrain*.
Preignition - Short for *premature ignition*. The premature burning of the air/fuel mixture in the combustion chamber, caused by combustion chamber heat and/or fuel instability. Preignition begins before the spark plug fires.

R

Relay - An electromechanical device which enables one circuit to open or close another circuit. A relay is usually operated by a low current circuit, but it controls the opening and closing of another circuit of higher current capacity.
Ring gap - The distance between the ends of the piston ring when installed in the cylinder.
rpm - Engine speed, measured in crankshaft *revolutions per minute*.

S

Scan Tool - A device that interfaces with and communicates information on a data link. Commonly used to get data from automotive computers.
Sending unit - Used to operate a gauge or indicator light. In indicator light circuits, contains contact points, like a switch. In gauge circuits, contains a variable resistance that modifies current flow in accordance with the condition or system being monitored.
Sensor - The generic name for a device that senses either the absolute value or a change in a physical quantity such as temperature, pressure, or flow rate, and converts that change into an electrical signal which is monitored by a computer.
Serpentine drivebelt - A single, long, wide accessory drivebelt that's used on some newer vehicles to drive all the accessories, instead of a series of smaller, shorter belts. Serpentine drivebelts are usually tensioned by an automatic tensioner.
Short block - An engine block complete with crankshaft and piston and, usually, camshaft assemblies.
Single-overhead cam (SOHC) - See *overhead cam*.
Spark gap - The space between the electrodes of a spark plug through which the spark jumps. Also, a safety device in a magneto to provide an alternate path for current when it exceeds a safe value.
Spark knock - See *detonation* or *preignition*.
Spark plug - An electrical device which protrudes into the combustion chamber of an engine. The spark plug contains an insulated center electrode for conducting high tension current from the distributor. This insulated electrode is spaced a predetermined distance from the side electrode to control the dimensions of the gap for the spark to jump across.
Stoichiometric - The ideal ratio of air to fuel, in terms of mass; results in the most complete and efficient combustion, converting the carbon and hydrogen content of the fuel into (mainly) water and carbon dioxide. The stoichiometric ratio varies with the heating value of the fuel: For example, it's around 15.1:1 by weight for 100-octane gasoline, 14.6:1 for regular, 9.0:1 to ethanol, 6.45:1 for methanol and so on.
Stroke - The distance the piston moves when traveling from top dead center to bottom dead center, or from bottom dead center to top dead center.
Sump - The lowest part of the oil pan. The part of oil pan that contains oil. See *oil pan*.
Supercharger - A mechanically-driven device that pressurizes the intake air, thereby increasing the density of charge air and the consequent power output from a given engine displacement. Superchargers are usually belt-driven by the engine crankshaft pulley. See *blower*.

T

Throttle body - On carburetors, the casting which houses the throttle plate(s) and shaft(s) and the throttle linkage for the primary and, if equipped, the secondary bores. The throttle body is a separate component that's bolted to the underside of the carburetor main body. On fuel-injection systems, the carburetor-like aluminum casting that houses the throttle valve, the idle air bypass (if equipped), the throttle position sensor (TPS), the idle air control (IAC) motor and, on TBI systems, one or two injectors.
Throttle Body Injection (TBI) - Any of several injection systems which have the fuel injector(s) mounted in a centrally located throttle body, as opposed to positioning the injectors close to the intake ports.
Throttle Position Sensor (TPS) - A potentiometric sensor that tells the computer the position (angle) of the throttle plate. The sensor wiper position is proportional to throttle position. The computer uses this information to control fuel flow.
Throw-out bearing - The bearing in the clutch assembly that is moved in to the release levers by clutch-pedal action to disengage the clutch. Also referred to as *release bearing*.
Timing marks (ignition) - Marks, usually located on the crankshaft pulley, used to synchronize the ignition system so the spark plugs will fire at the correct time.
Timing marks (valves) - Marks placed on the crankshaft and camshaft sprockets or gears which must be aligned with their corresponding marks so that the camshaft(s) and crankshaft are synchronized.
Torque - A turning or twisting force, such as the force imparted on a fastener by a torque wrench. Usually expressed in foot-pounds (ft-lbs).
Turbocharger - A centrifugal device, driven by exhaust gases, that pressurizes the intake air, thereby increasing the density of the charge air, and therefore the resulting power output, from a given engine displacement.

V

Valve clearance - The clearance between the valve tip (the end of the valve stem) and the rocker arm. The valve clearance is measured when the valve is closed.
Valve float - The condition which occurs when the valves are forced back open before they've had a chance to seat. Valve float is usually caused by extremely high rpm.
Valve grinding - The process of refacing a valve in a valve refacing machine.
Valve guide - The cast-iron bore that's part of the head, or the bronze or silicon-bronze tube that's pressed into the head, to provide support and lubrication for the valve stem.
Valve head - The portion of a valve upon which the valve face is machined.
Valve keeper - Also referred to as valve key. Small half-cylinder of steel that snaps into a groove in the upper end of valve stem. Two keepers per valve are used. Designed to secure valve spring, valve retainer and valve stem together. Also referred to as a *valve key* or *valve lock*.
Valve lifter - A cylindrical device that contacts the end of the cam lobe and the lower end of the pushrod. The lifter rides on the camshaft. When the cam lobe moves it upward, it pushes on the pushrod, which pushes on the lifer and opens the valve. Also referred to as a *lifter*, *tappet*, *valve tappet* or *cam follower*.
Valve overlap - The number of degrees of crankshaft rotation during which both the intake and the exhaust valve are partially open (the intake is starting to open while the exhaust is not yet closed).
Valve stem - The long, thin, cylindrical bearing surface of the valve that slides up and down in the valve guide.

W

Wastegate - A device which bleeds off exhaust gases before they reach the turbocharger when boost pressure reaches a set limit.
Water pump - A pump, usually mounted on the front of the engine and driven by an accessory drivebelt, which forces coolant through the cooling system.
White smoke - Unburned fuel emitted by the exhaust that indicates low combustion chamber temperatures.
Wrist pin - A journal for bearing in small end of an engine connecting rod which also passes through piston walls. See *piston pin*.

Source List

AEM (Advanced Engine Management)
2205 126th St., Unit A
Hawthorne, CA 90250
(310) 484-2322
www.aempower.com

APC (American Products Company)
22324 Temescal Canyon Rd.
Corona, CA 92883
(909) 898-9840
www.4apc.com

A'PEX Integration
(intercoolers, intakes, blow-off valves, more)
330 West Taft
Orange, CA 92865
(714) 685-5700
www.apexi.com

B&M Racing and Performance Parts
(fuel system and many other parts)
9142 Independence Ave.
Chatsworth, CA 91311
(818) 882-6422
www.bmracing.com

Blitz
(intakes, turbo components, other parts)
4879 East La Palma Ave., Suite 202
Anaheim, CA 92807
(714) 777-9766
www.blitz-na.com

Competition Cams
(cams, valvetrain parts, ZEX nitrous kits)
3406 Democrat Road
Memphis, TN 38118
(888) 817-1008
www.zex.com

Clutch Masters
267 E. Valley Blvd.
Rialto, CA 92376
(909) 877-6800
www.clutchmasters.com

Crane Cams
530 Fentress Blvd.
Daytona Beach, FL 32114
(386) 258-6174
www.cranecams.com

DC Sports
(cold air intakes, exhausts, other parts)
1451 East 6th Street
Corona, CA 92879
(909) 734-2020
www.dcsports.com

Edelbrock Corp.
(intake components, nitrous)
2700 California Street
Torrance, CA 90503
(310) 781-2222
www.edelbrock.com

Flexalite
(FAL fans)
P.O. Box 580
Milton, WA 98354
(253) 922-2700
www.flex-a-lite.com

Fluidyne
(aluminum radiators)
2605 East Cedar St.
Ontario, CA 91761
(800) 358-4396
www.fluidyne.com

Focus Sport
1350 N. Hundley St.
Anaheim, CA 92806
(714) 630-6353
www.focussport.com

Ford Racing Performance Parts
(Ford sport compact catalog)
P.O. Box 51394
Livonia, MI 48151
(586) 468-1356
www.performanceparts.ford.com

Grant Products
700 Allen Ave.
Glendale, CA 91201
(818) 247-2910
www.grantproducts.com

GReddy Performance Products
(large catalog of performance parts)
9 Vanderbilt
Irvine, CA 92618
(949) 588-8300
www.greddy.com

Grillcraft Sport Grilles
11651 Prairie Ave.
Hawthorne, CA 90250
(310) 970-0300
www.grillcraft.com

Gude
(camshafts, valvetrain, ported heads)
29885 2nd St., Suite Q
Lake Elsinore, CA 92530
www.gude.com

Holley Performance Products
(Airmass Exhaust, Holley Ignition, NOS, Earl's)
1801 Russellville Road, P.O. Box 10360
Bowling Green, KY 42102-7360
(800) Holley-1
www.holley.com

Innovative Turbo Systems
845 Easy Street
Simi Valley, CA 93065
(805) 526-5400
www.innovativeturbo.com

Jackson Racing
(supercharger kits and more)
440 Rutherford Street
Goleta, CA 93117
(888) 888-4079
www.jacksonracing.com

Jacobs Electronics
2519 Dana Drive
Laurinburg, NC 28352
(800) 782-3379
www.jacobselectronics.com

JE Pistons
15312 Connector Lane
Huntington Beach, CA 92649
(714) 898-9763
www.jepistons.com

JL Audio, Inc.
(Amplifiers, speakers, subwoofers)
10369 N. Commerce Parkway
Miramar, FL 33025
(954) 443-1100
www.jlaudio.com

K&N Engineering
(air filters, intake kits)
P.O. Box 1329
Riverside, CA 92502
(888) 949-1832
www.knfilters.com

Lokar Motorsports
10924 Murdock Dr.
Knoxville, TN 37932
(865) 966-2269
www.lokarmotorsports.com

Midnight Performance
(import tuning shop, products)
3324 Monier Circle, #1 and 2
Rancho Cordova, CA 95742
(916) 852-6887
www.midnightperformance.com

Moore Performance
(racing driveline components)
3740 Greenwood Street
San Diego, CA 92110
(619) 296-9180

MSD
(ignition products)
1490 Henry Brennan Drive
El Paso, TX 79936
(915) 857-5200
www.msdignition.com

Nitrous Express (NX)
1808 Southwest Parkway
Wichita Falls, TX 76302
(888) 463-2781
www.nitrousexpress.com

Source List

NOS
(see Holley)

ProDrive
(driveline components)
6530 Alondra Blvd.
Paramount, CA 90723
(888) 340-4753
www.prodriveusa.com

Racers Against Street Racing (RASR)
A coalition of auto manufacturers, aftermarket parts companies, professional drag racers, sanctioning bodies, race tracks and automotive magazines devoted to promoting safe and legal alternatives to illegal street racing on a national level. The message is simple: If you want to race, go to a racetrack!
www.racersagainststreetracing.org

RC Engineering
(injectors, injection specialists)
1728 Border Avenue
Torrance, CA 90501
(310) 320-2277
www.rceng.com

Saleen Performance
76 Fairbanks
Irvine, CA 92618
(949) 597-4900
www.Saleen.com

SAVV Mobile Multimedia
(mobile video)
15348 Garfield Ave.
Paramount, CA 90723
(562) 529-7700
www.savv.com

Scosche
1550 Pacific Ave.
Oxnard, CA 93033
1-800-621-3695
www.scosche.com

SSP/Street Sound Plus
2751 Thousand Oaks Blvd.
Thousand Oaks, CA 91362
(805) 557-1054

Steeda Autosports
2241 Hammondville Rd.
Pompano Beach, FL 33069
(954) 960-0774
www.steeda.com

Turbo Specialties
(turbo kits)
17906 Crusader Avenue
Cerritos, CA 90703
(562) 403-7039

Turbonetics
(turbochargers)
2255 Agate Court
Simi Valley, CA 93065
(805) 581-0333
www.turboneticsinc.com

Veilside USA
(performance and appearance parts)
1250 E. 223rd St., #105
Carson, CA 90745
(310) 835-5684
www.veilside.com

Vortech Engineering
(supercharger kits)
1650 Pacific Avenue
Channel islands, CA 93033
(805) 247-0226
www.vortechsuperchargers.com

Woodview
5670 Timberlea Blvd.
Mississauga, Ontario Canada
L4W 4M6
1-800-797-DASH (3274)
www.woodcorp.com

ZEX
(nitrous oxide kits)
3406 Democrat Road
Memphis, TN 38118
(888) 817-1008
www.zex.com

A special thanks to:

- APC (American Products Company), Focus Sport, Grillcraft, Grant Products, JL Audio, Lokar Motorsports, MSD and Woodview for supplying many of the custom and performance parts seen throughout this book.
- Lucette Nicoll of Nicoll Public Relations for arranging much of the in-vehicle entertainment content.
- Phil Weitzl (Universal Products)
- Robin Girard (Woodview)
- Nathan Perkins and Manuel Gomez (Scosche)
- Jaime (Dracula) Palafox and Hector Galvan at SSP (Street Sound Plus), Thousand Oaks for all the Mobile Entertainment installations.
- Dave Klienbach
- Ramon Cuguas

HAYNES REPAIR MANUALS

ACURA
- *12020 Integra '86 thru '89 & Legend '86 thru '90
- 12021 Integra '90 thru '93 & Legend '91 thru '95

AMC
- Jeep CJ - see JEEP (50020)
- 14020 Mid-size models '70 thru '83
- 14025 (Renault) Alliance & Encore '83 thru '87

AUDI
- 15020 4000 all models '80 thru '87
- 15025 5000 all models '77 thru '83
- 15026 5000 all models '84 thru '88

AUSTIN-HEALEY
- Sprite - see MG Midget (66015)

BMW
- *18020 3/5 Series not including diesel or all-wheel drive models '82 thru '92
- 18021 3-Series incl. Z3 models '92 thru '98
- 18025 320i all 4 cyl models '75 thru '83
- 18050 1500 thru 2002 except Turbo '59 thru '77

BUICK
- *19010 Buick Century '97 thru '02
- Century (front-wheel drive) - see GM (38005)
- *19020 Buick, Oldsmobile & Pontiac Full-size (Front-wheel drive) '85 thru '02
  - Buick Electra, LeSabre and Park Avenue; Oldsmobile Delta 88 Royale, Ninety Eight and Regency; Pontiac Bonneville
- 19025 Buick Oldsmobile & Pontiac Full-size (Rear wheel drive)
  - Buick Estate '70 thru '90, Electra'70 thru '84, LeSabre '70 thru '85, Limited '74 thru '79
  - Oldsmobile Custom Cruiser '70 thru '90, Delta 88 '70 thru '85,Ninety-eight '70 thru '84
  - Pontiac Bonneville '70 thru '81, Catalina '70 thru '81, Grandville '70 thru '75, Parisienne '83 thru '86
- 19030 Mid-size Regal & Century all rear-drive models with V6, V8 and Turbo '74 thru '87
  - Regal - see GENERAL MOTORS (38010)
  - Riviera - see GENERAL MOTORS (38030)
  - Roadmaster - see CHEVROLET (24046)
  - Skyhawk - see GENERAL MOTORS (38015)
  - Skylark - see GM (38020, 38025)
  - Somerset - see GENERAL MOTORS (38025)

CADILLAC
- 21030 Cadillac Rear Wheel Drive all gasoline models '70 thru '93
- Cimarron - see GENERAL MOTORS (38015)
- DeVille - see GM (38031 & 38032)
- Eldorado - see GM (38030 & 38031)
- Fleetwood - see GM (38031)
- Seville - see GM (38030, 38031 & 38032)

CHEVROLET
- *24010 Astro & GMC Safari Mini-vans '85 thru '02
- 24015 Camaro V8 all models '70 thru '81
- 24016 Camaro all models '82 thru '92
- 24017 Camaro & Firebird '93 thru '00
- Cavalier - see GENERAL MOTORS (38016)
- Celebrity - see GENERAL MOTORS (38005)
- 24020 Chevelle, Malibu & El Camino '69 thru '87
- 24024 Chevette & Pontiac T1000 '76 thru '87
- Citation - see GENERAL MOTORS (38020)
- 24032 Corsica/Beretta all models '87 thru '96
- 24040 Corvette all V8 models '68 thru '82
- 24041 Corvette all models '84 thru '96
- 10305 Chevrolet Engine Overhaul Manual
- 24045 Full-size Sedans Caprice, Impala, Biscayne, Bel Air & Wagons '69 thru '90
- 24046 Impala SS & Caprice and Buick Roadmaster '91 thru '96
- Impala - see LUMINA (24048)
- Lumina '90 thru '94 - see GM (38010)
- *24048 Lumina & Monte Carlo '95 thru '01
- Lumina APV - see GM (38035)
- *24050 Luv Pick-up all 2WD & 4WD '72 thru '82
- Malibu '97 thru '00 - see GM (38026)
- 24055 Monte Carlo all models '70 thru '88
- Monte Carlo '95 thru '01 - see LUMINA (24048)
- 24059 Nova all V8 models '69 thru '79
- 24060 Nova and Geo Prizm '85 thru '92
- 24064 Pick-ups '67 thru '87 - Chevrolet & GMC, all V8 & in-line 6 cyl, 2WD & 4WD '67 thru '87; Suburbans, Blazers & Jimmys '67 thru '91
- *24065 Pick-ups '88 thru '98 - Chevrolet & GMC, full-size pick-ups '88 thru '98, C/K Classic '99 & '00, Blazer & Jimmy '92 thru '94; Suburban '92 thru '99; Tahoe & Yukon '95 thru '99
- *24066 Pick-ups '99 thru '02 - Chevrolet Silverado & GMC Sierra full-size pick-ups '99 thru '03, Suburban/Tahoe/Yukon/Yukon XL '00 thru '02
- 24070 S-10 & S-15 Pick-ups '82 thru '93, Blazer & Jimmy '83 thru '94,
- *24071 S-10 & S-15 Pick-ups '94 thru '01, Blazer & Jimmy '95 thru '01, Hombre '96 thru '01
- *24072 Chevrolet TrailBlazer & TrailBlazer EXT, GMC Envoy & Envoy XL, Oldsmobile Bravada '02 and '03
- 24075 Sprint '85 thru '88 & Geo Metro '89 thru '01
- 24080 Vans - Chevrolet & GMC '68 thru '96

CHRYSLER
- 25015 Chrysler Cirrus, Dodge Stratus, Plymouth Breeze '95 thru '00
- 10310 Chrysler Engine Overhaul Manual
- 25020 Full-size Front-Wheel Drive '88 thru '93
- K-Cars - see DODGE Aries (30008)
- Laser - see DODGE Daytona (30030)
- 25025 Chrysler LHS, Concorde, New Yorker, Dodge Intrepid, Eagle Vision, '93 thru '97
- *25026 Chrysler LHS, Concorde, 300M, Dodge Intrepid, '98 thru '03
- 25030 Chrysler & Plymouth Mid-size front wheel drive '82 thru '95
- Rear-wheel Drive - see Dodge (30050)
- *25035 PT Cruiser all models '01 thru '03
- *25040 Chrysler Sebring, Dodge Avenger '95 thru '02

DATSUN
- 28005 200SX all models '80 thru '83
- 28007 B-210 all models '73 thru '78
- 28009 210 all models '79 thru '82
- 28012 240Z, 260Z & 280Z Coupe '70 thru '78
- 28014 280ZX Coupe & 2+2 '79 thru '83
- 300ZX - see NISSAN (72010)
- 28016 310 all models '78 thru '82
- 28018 510 & PL521 Pick-up '68 thru '73
- 28020 510 all models '78 thru '81
- 28022 620 Series Pick-up all models '73 thru '79
- 720 Series Pick-up - see NISSAN (72030)
- 28025 810/Maxima all gasoline models, '77 thru '84

DODGE
- 400 & 600 - see CHRYSLER (25030)
- 30008 Aries & Plymouth Reliant '81 thru '89
- 30010 Caravan & Plymouth Voyager '84 thru '95
- *30011 Caravan & Plymouth Voyager '96 thru '02
- 30012 Challenger/Plymouth Saporro '78 thru '83
- 30016 Colt & Plymouth Champ '78 thru '87
- 30020 Dakota Pick-ups all models '87 thru '96
- *30021 Durango '98 & '99, Dakota '97 thru '99
- 30025 Dart, Demon, Plymouth Barracuda, Duster & Valiant 6 cyl models '67 thru '76
- 30030 Daytona & Chrysler Laser '84 thru '89
- Intrepid - see CHRYSLER (25025, 25026)
- *30034 Neon all models '95 thru '99
- 30035 Omni & Plymouth Horizon '78 thru '90
- 30040 Pick-ups all full-size models '74 thru '93
- *30041 Pick-ups all full-size models '94 thru '01
- 30045 Ram 50/D50 Pick-ups & Raider and Plymouth Arrow Pick-ups '79 thru '93
- 30050 Dodge/Plymouth/Chrysler RWD '71 thru '89
- 30055 Shadow & Plymouth Sundance '87 thru '94
- 30060 Spirit & Plymouth Acclaim '89 thru '95
- *30065 Vans - Dodge & Plymouth '71 thru '03

EAGLE
- Talon - see MITSUBISHI (68030, 68031)
- Vision - see CHRYSLER (25025)

FIAT
- 34010 124 Sport Coupe & Spider '68 thru '78
- 34025 X1/9 all models '74 thru '80

FORD
- 10355 Ford Automatic Transmission Overhaul
- 36004 Aerostar Mini-vans all models '86 thru '97
- 36006 Contour & Mercury Mystique '95 thru '00
- 36008 Courier Pick-up all models '72 thru '82
- *36012 Crown Victoria & Mercury Grand Marquis '88 thru '00
- 10320 Ford Engine Overhaul Manual
- 36016 Escort/Mercury Lynx all models '81 thru '90
- 36020 Escort/Mercury Tracer '91 thru '00
- 36022 Ford Escape and Mazda Tribute '01 thru '03
- 36024 Explorer & Mazda Navajo '91 thru '01
- 36028 Fairmont & Mercury Zephyr '78 thru '83
- 36030 Festiva & Aspire '88 thru '97
- 36032 Fiesta all models '77 thru '80
- *36034 Focus all models '00 and '01
- 36036 Ford & Mercury Full-size '75 thru '87
- 36044 Ford & Mercury Mid-size '75 thru '86
- 36048 Mustang V8 all models '64-1/2 thru '73
- 36049 Mustang II 4 cyl, V6 & V8 models '74 thru '78
- 36050 Mustang & Mercury Capri all models Mustang, '79 thru '93; Capri, '79 thru '86
- *36051 Mustang all models '94 thru '03
- 36054 Pick-ups & Bronco '73 thru '79
- 36058 Pick-ups & Bronco '80 thru '96
- *36059 F-150 & Expedition '97 thru '02, F-250 '97 thru '99 & Lincoln Navigator '98 thru '02
- *36060 Super Duty Pick-ups, Excursion '97 thru '02
- 36062 Pinto & Mercury Bobcat '75 thru '80
- 36066 Probe all models '89 thru '92
- 36070 Ranger/Bronco II gasoline models '83 thru '92
- *36071 Ranger '93 thru '00 & Mazda Pick-ups '94 thru '00
- 36074 Taurus & Mercury Sable '86 thru '95
- *36075 Taurus & Mercury Sable '96 thru '01
- 36078 Tempo & Mercury Topaz '84 thru '94
- 36082 Thunderbird/Mercury Cougar '83 thru '88
- 36086 Thunderbird/Mercury Cougar '89 and '97
- 36090 Vans all V8 Econoline models '69 thru '91
- *36094 Vans full size '92 thru '01
- *36097 Windstar Mini-van '95 thru '03

GENERAL MOTORS
- 10360 GM Automatic Transmission Overhaul
- 38005 Buick Century, Chevrolet Celebrity, Oldsmobile Cutlass Ciera & Pontiac 6000 all models '82 thru '96
- *38010 Buick Regal, Chevrolet Lumina, Oldsmobile Cutlass Supreme & Pontiac Grand Prix (FWD) '88 thru '02
- 38015 Buick Skyhawk, Cadillac Cimarron, Chevrolet Cavalier, Oldsmobile Firenza & Pontiac J-2000 & Sunbird '82 thru '94
- *38016 Chevrolet Cavalier & Pontiac Sunfire '95 thru '01
- 38020 Buick Skylark, Chevrolet Citation, Olds Omega, Pontiac Phoenix '80 thru '85
- 38025 Buick Skylark & Somerset, Oldsmobile Achieva & Calais and Pontiac Grand Am models '85 thru '98
- *38026 Chevrolet Malibu, Olds Alero & Cutlass, Pontiac Grand Am '97 thru '00
- 38030 Cadillac Eldorado '71 thru '85, Seville '80 thru '85, Oldsmobile Toronado '71 thru '85, Buick Riviera '79 thru '85
- *38031 Cadillac Eldorado & Seville '86 thru '91, DeVille '86 thru '93, Fleetwood & Olds Toronado '86 thru '92, Buick Riviera '86 thru '93
- 38032 Cadillac DeVille '94 thru '02 & Seville - '92 thru '02
- 38035 Chevrolet Lumina APV, Olds Silhouette & Pontiac Trans Sport all models '90 thru '96
- *38036 Chevrolet Venture, Olds Silhouette, Pontiac Trans Sport & Montana '97 thru '01
- General Motors Full-size Rear-wheel Drive - see BUICK (19025)

* Listings shown with an asterisk (*) indicate model coverage as of this printing. These titles will be periodically updated to include later model years - consult your Haynes dealer for more information.

Haynes North America, Inc., 861 Lawrence Drive, Newbury Park, CA 91320-1514 • (805) 498-6703

HAYNES Repair Manuals

GEO
- **Metro** - see CHEVROLET Sprint (24075)
- **Prizm** - '85 thru '92 see CHEVY (24060), '93 thru '02 see TOYOTA Corolla (92036)
- 40030 **Storm** all models '90 thru '93
- **Tracker** - see SUZUKI Samurai (90010)

GMC
- **Vans & Pick-ups** - see CHEVROLET

HONDA
- 42010 **Accord CVCC** all models '76 thru '83
- 42011 **Accord** all models '84 thru '89
- 42012 **Accord** all models '90 thru '93
- 42013 **Accord** all models '94 thru '97
- *42014 **Accord** all models '98 and '99
- 42020 **Civic 1200** all models '73 thru '79
- 42021 **Civic 1300 & 1500 CVCC** '80 thru '83
- 42022 **Civic 1500 CVCC** all models '75 thru '79
- 42023 **Civic** all models '84 thru '91
- 42024 **Civic & del Sol** '92 thru '95
- *42025 **Civic** '96 thru '00, **CR-V** '97 thru '00, **Acura Integra** '94 thru '00
- 42040 **Prelude CVCC** all models '79 thru '89

HYUNDAI
- *43010 **Elantra** all models '96 thru '01
- 43015 **Excel & Accent** all models '86 thru '98

ISUZU
- **Hombre** - see CHEVROLET S-10 (24071)
- *47017 **Rodeo** '91 thru '02; **Amigo** '89 thru '94 and '98 thru '02; **Honda Passport** '95 thru '02
- 47020 **Trooper & Pick-up** '81 thru '93

JAGUAR
- 49010 **XJ6** all 6 cyl models '68 thru '86
- 49011 **XJ6** all models '88 thru '94
- 49015 **XJ12 & XJS** all 12 cyl models '72 thru '85

JEEP
- 50010 **Cherokee, Comanche & Wagoneer Limited** all models '84 thru '00
- 50020 **CJ** all models '49 thru '86
- *50025 **Grand Cherokee** all models '93 thru '00
- 50029 **Grand Wagoneer & Pick-up** '72 thru '91 Grand Wagoneer '84 thru '91, Cherokee & Wagoneer '72 thru '83, Pick-up '72 thru '88
- *50030 **Wrangler** all models '87 thru '00

LEXUS
- **ES 300** - see TOYOTA Camry (92007)

LINCOLN
- **Navigator** - see FORD Pick-up (36059)
- *59010 **Rear-Wheel Drive** all models '70 thru '01

MAZDA
- 61010 **GLC Hatchback** (rear-wheel drive) '77 thru '83
- 61011 **GLC** (front-wheel drive) '81 thru '85
- 61015 **323 & Protegé** '90 thru '00
- *61016 **MX-5 Miata** '90 thru '97
- 61020 **MPV** all models '89 thru '94
- **Navajo** - see Ford Explorer (36024)
- 61030 **Pick-ups** '72 thru '93
- **Pick-ups** '94 thru '00 - see Ford Ranger (36071)
- 61035 **RX-7** all models '79 thru '85
- 61036 **RX-7** all models '86 thru '91
- 61040 **626** (rear-wheel drive) all models '79 thru '82
- 61041 **626/MX-6** (front-wheel drive) '83 thru '91
- 61042 **626** '93 thru '01, **MX-6/Ford Probe** '93 thru '97

MERCEDES-BENZ
- 63012 **123 Series Diesel** '76 thru '85
- 63015 **190 Series** four-cyl gas models, '84 thru '88
- 63020 **230/250/280** 6 cyl sohc models '68 thru '72
- 63025 **280 123 Series** gasoline models '77 thru '81
- 63030 **350 & 450** all models '71 thru '80

MERCURY
- 64200 **Villager & Nissan Quest** '93 thru '01
- All other titles, see FORD Listing.

MG
- 66010 **MGB** Roadster & GT Coupe '62 thru '80
- 66015 **MG Midget, Austin Healey Sprite** '58 thru '80

MITSUBISHI
- 68020 **Cordia, Tredia, Galant, Precis & Mirage** '83 thru '93
- 68030 **Eclipse, Eagle Talon & Ply. Laser** '90 thru '94
- *68031 **Eclipse** '95 thru '01, **Eagle Talon** '95 thru '98
- 68035 **Mitsubishi Galant** - 1994 through 2003
- 68040 **Pick-up** '83 thru '96 & **Montero** '83 thru '93

NISSAN
- 72010 **300ZX** all models including Turbo '84 thru '89
- 72015 **Altima** all models '93 thru '01
- 72020 **Maxima** all models '85 thru '92
- 72021 **Maxima** all models '93 thru '01
- 72030 **Pick-ups** '80 thru '97 **Pathfinder** '87 thru '95
- *72031 **Frontier Pick-up** '98 thru '01, **Xterra** '00 & '01, **Pathfinder** '96 thru '01
- 72040 **Pulsar** all models '83 thru '86
- **Quest** - see MERCURY Villager (64200)
- 72050 **Sentra** all models '82 thru '94
- 72051 **Sentra & 200SX** all models '95 thru '99
- 72060 **Stanza** all models '82 thru '90

OLDSMOBILE
- 73015 **Cutlass** V6 & V8 gas models '74 thru '88
- For other OLDSMOBILE titles, see BUICK, CHEVROLET or GENERAL MOTORS listing.

PLYMOUTH
- For PLYMOUTH titles, see DODGE listing.

PONTIAC
- 79008 **Fiero** all models '84 thru '88
- 79018 **Firebird** V8 models except Turbo '70 thru '81
- 79019 **Firebird** all models '82 thru '92
- 79040 **Mid-size Rear-wheel Drive** '70 thru '87
- For other PONTIAC titles, see BUICK, CHEVROLET or GENERAL MOTORS listing.

PORSCHE
- 80020 **911** except Turbo & Carrera 4 '65 thru '89
- 80025 **914** all 4 cyl models '69 thru '76
- 80030 **924** all models including Turbo '76 thru '82
- 80035 **944** all models including Turbo '83 thru '89

RENAULT
- **Alliance & Encore** - see AMC (14020)

SAAB
- *84010 **900** all models including Turbo '79 thru '88

SATURN
- *87010 **Saturn** all models '91 thru '02

SUBARU
- 89002 **1100, 1300, 1400 & 1600** '71 thru '79
- 89003 **1600 & 1800** 2WD & 4WD '80 thru '94

SUZUKI
- 90010 **Samurai/Sidekick & Geo Tracker** '86 thru '01

TOYOTA
- 92005 **Camry** all models '83 thru '91
- 92006 **Camry** all models '92 thru '96
- *92007 **Camry, Avalon, Solara, Lexus ES 300** '97 thru '01
- 92015 **Celica Rear Wheel Drive** '71 thru '85
- 92020 **Celica Front Wheel Drive** '86 thru '99
- 92025 **Celica Supra** all models '79 thru '92
- 92030 **Corolla** all models '75 thru '79
- 92032 **Corolla** all rear wheel drive models '80 thru '87
- 92035 **Corolla** all front wheel drive models '84 thru '92
- 92036 **Corolla & Geo Prizm** '93 thru '02
- 92040 **Corolla Tercel** all models '80 thru '82
- 92045 **Corona** all models '74 thru '82
- 92050 **Cressida** all models '78 thru '82
- 92055 **Land Cruiser FJ40, 43, 45, 55** '68 thru '82
- 92056 **Land Cruiser FJ60, 62, 80, FZJ80** '80 thru '96
- 92065 **MR2** all models '85 thru '87
- 92070 **Pick-up** all models '69 thru '78
- 92075 **Pick-up** all models '79 thru '95
- *92076 **Tacoma** '95 thru '00, **4Runner** '96 thru '00, & **T100** '93 thru '98
- *92078 **Tundra** '00 thru '02 & **Sequoia** '01 thru '02
- 92080 **Previa** all models '91 thru '95
- *92082 **RAV4** all models '96 thru '02
- 92085 **Tercel** all models '87 thru '94

TRIUMPH
- 94007 **Spitfire** all models '62 thru '81
- 94010 **TR7** all models '75 thru '81

VW
- 96008 **Beetle & Karmann Ghia** '54 thru '79
- *96009 **New Beetle** '98 thru '00
- 96016 **Rabbit, Jetta, Scirocco & Pick-up** gas models '74 thru '91 & Convertible '80 thru '92
- 96017 **Golf, GTI & Jetta** '93 thru '98 & **Cabrio** '95 thru '98
- *96018 **Golf, GTI, Jetta & Cabrio** '99 thru '02
- 96020 **Rabbit, Jetta & Pick-up** diesel '77 thru '84
- 96023 **Passat** '98 thru '01, **Audi A4** '96 thru '01
- 96030 **Transporter 1600** all models '68 thru '79
- 96035 **Transporter 1700, 1800 & 2000** '72 thru '79
- 96040 **Type 3 1500 & 1600** all models '63 thru '73
- 96045 **Vanagon** all air-cooled models '80 thru '83

VOLVO
- 97010 **120, 130 Series & 1800 Sports** '61 thru '73
- 97015 **140 Series** all models '66 thru '74
- 97020 **240 Series** all models '76 thru '93
- 97040 **740 & 760 Series** all models '82 thru '88
- 97050 **850 Series** all models '93 thru '97

TECHBOOK MANUALS
- 10205 **Automotive Computer Codes**
- 10210 **Automotive Emissions Control Manual**
- 10215 **Fuel Injection Manual, 1978 thru 1985**
- 10220 **Fuel Injection Manual, 1986 thru 1999**
- 10225 **Holley Carburetor Manual**
- 10230 **Rochester Carburetor Manual**
- 10240 **Weber/Zenith/Stromberg/SU Carburetors**
- 10305 **Chevrolet Engine Overhaul Manual**
- 10310 **Chrysler Engine Overhaul Manual**
- 10320 **Ford Engine Overhaul Manual**
- 10330 **GM and Ford Diesel Engine Repair Manual**
- 10340 **Small Engine Repair Manual, 5 HP & Less**
- 10341 **Small Engine Repair Manual, 5.5 - 20 HP**
- 10345 **Suspension, Steering & Driveline Manual**
- 10355 **Ford Automatic Transmission Overhaul**
- 10360 **GM Automatic Transmission Overhaul**
- 10405 **Automotive Body Repair & Painting**
- 10410 **Automotive Brake Manual**
- 10411 **Automotive Anti-lock Brake (ABS) Systems**
- 10415 **Automotive Detailing Manual**
- 10420 **Automotive Eelectrical Manual**
- 10425 **Automotive Heating & Air Conditioning**
- 10430 **Automotive Reference Manual & Dictionary**
- 10435 **Automotive Tools Manual**
- 10440 **Used Car Buying Guide**
- 10445 **Welding Manual**
- 10450 **ATV Basics**

SPANISH MANUALS
- 98903 **Reparación de Carrocería & Pintura**
- 98905 **Códigos Automotrices de la Computadora**
- 98910 **Frenos Automotriz**
- 98915 **Inyección de Combustible 1986 al 1999**
- 99040 **Chevrolet & GMC Camionetas** '67 al '87 Incluye Suburban, Blazer & Jimmy '67 al '91
- 99041 **Chevrolet & GMC Camionetas** '88 al '98 Incluye Suburban '92 al '98, Blazer & Jimmy '92 al '94, Tahoe y Yukon '95 al '98
- 99042 **Chevrolet & GMC Camionetas Cerradas** '68 al '95
- 99055 **Dodge Caravan & Plymouth Voyager** '84 al '95
- 99075 **Ford Camionetas y Bronco** '80 al '94
- 99077 **Ford Camionetas Cerradas** '69 al '91
- 99083 **Ford Modelos de Tamaño Grande** '75 al '87
- 99088 **Ford Modelos de Tamaño Mediano** '75 al '86
- 99091 **Ford Taurus & Mercury Sable** '86 al '95
- 99095 **GM Modelos de Tamaño Grande** '70 al '90
- 99100 **GM Modelos de Tamaño Mediano** '70 al '88
- 99110 **Nissan Camioneta** '80 al '96, **Pathfinder** '87 al '95
- 99118 **Nissan Sentra** '82 al '94
- 99125 **Toyota Camionetas y 4Runner** '79 al '95

* Listings shown with an asterisk (*) indicate model coverage as of this printing. These titles will be periodically updated to include later model years - consult your Haynes dealer for more information.

Haynes North America, Inc., 861 Lawrence Drive, Newbury Park, CA 91320-1514 • (805) 498-6703